Mighty *to* Save

M000191677

206 CONTRAST(C ... MAN ...

Devil's Power + Arena

207 MIRACLES AS ILLUS OF LOST

113 ⑤

MIRACULOUS HEALINGS NOT NEARLY AS IMPORTANT

P.115 ... ...

AS SPIR. HEALINGS

LK 2:14

YET MANY PRAY MORE FOR IT

P43

P64 FAITH

185 AGNOSTICISM

P45

Leprosy (3110)

P 23 etc.

X TRUTH — SP. WEAPON AGAINST DEVIL P.181

P 8 V 9

(II)

53 →
Self
esteem

✗ We are better
off from
Adam. We
can't
lose our
righteousness

216
I WILLS
OF
CHRIST

(136)

GOD MUST PUNISH
SIN — LIKE A
HUMAN JUDGE
IT WOULD BE
WRONG NOT TO
DO — PUTS RESTRAINT
ON SIN & THAT
IS GOOD

GOOD THAT
THERE IS
WARNING RE
HELL

Mighty *to* Save

DISCOVERING

GOD'S GRACE

IN THE

MIRACLES

OF JESUS

Richard D. Phillips

P&R

PUBLISHING

P.O. BOX 817 • PHILLIPSBURG • NEW JERSEY 08865-0817

Page design by Tobias Design
Typesetting by Michelle Feaster

Printed in the United States of America

Library of Congress Cataloging-in-Publication Data

Phillips, Richard D. (Richard Davis), 1960-
    Mighty to save : discovering God's grace in the miracles
of Jesus / Richard D. Phillips.
        p. cm.
    Includes bibliographical references and index.
    ISBN 0-87552-184-3 (pbk.)
    1. Jesus Christ—Miracles. 2. Bible. N.T. Luke—Theology.
3. Christian life—Presbyterian authors. I. Title.

BT366.3 .P47 2001
226.7'06—dc21

                                        00-068104

TO SHARON

Beloved wife, partner in life, sister in Christ

(Proverbs 31:10–11)

and

TO HIM

Robed in splendor,
striding forth in the greatness of his strength,
speaking in righteousness, mighty to save.

(Isaiah 63:1)

ALL OTHER
RELIGIONS
SHOW NO MIRACLES
P1

1910-?

Contents

R/ruder, although
I thought he kept
10 COMM. had no
peace

Preface

We are living in a time dominated by a focus on the self. Christians recognize the self-centeredness that so defines the worldly culture around us. Few of us, however, reflect on the way this kind of thinking has shaped our own view of the Christian life and salvation. How many Christians center their assurance, their peace, their power in their own performance? Having been saved by faith we would live by our works. This way of thinking is a recipe for a dwarfish Christianity, which is precisely what so many of us experience.

The antidote for this problem, of course, is a fresh gaze upon our Lord Jesus Christ. In particular, as I hope to show in this book, a grasp of the sufficiency of his work is the answer for our need. Jesus came to accomplish a work set before him by the Father (see John 17:4), a work of redemption by way of the cross. The various miracles he performed along the way inform us of that greater work, and they anticipate its ultimate effects when all of his and our enemies will be put away. They also tell of his willingness to help us now, the power that is available to us for righteousness, peace, and joy. It is my prayer that through these studies you will come to a firmer grasp of what Jesus has accomplished for all who look to him in faith and therefore to a stronger hope in which to live.

I have many people to thank with regard to this book. First, I thank my family for their forbearance, prayers, and help, and especially my wife, Sharon, to whom this book is dedicated with love. Second, I want to thank my friends Bruce Bell, Lee Beckham, and Jen Brewer for kindly reading these chapters and making helpful suggestions that have improved the book significantly. I am reminded of my debt of gratitude to Dr. Vern S. Poythress, professor of New Testament interpretation at Westminster Theological Seminary, with hopes that he will find this book a credit to his excellent instruction on the miracles of Christ. I am especially indebted to the late Dr. James Montgomery Boice, whose example, encouragement, and support has been so powerful a force in my life and ministry. Finally, I give my heartfelt thanks to the session and congregation of Tenth Presbyterian Church in Philadelphia, to whom these messages first were preached and whose prayers and love are more precious to me than gold.

The Meaning of the Miracles

Luke 4:14–44

*He has sent me to proclaim freedom for the prisoners
and recovery of sight for the blind, to release the oppressed,
to proclaim the year of the Lord's favor. (LUKE 4:18–19)*

In *Miracles*, English writer C. S. Lewis observed that miracles are essential to Christianity in a manner that is not true of any other religious system. Hinduism or Buddhism or Islam does not require us to step out of the bounds of nature. Christianity differs from these in that it posits a world that in its natural state is lost, that requires an inbreaking of divine power and action for salvation. The Bible teaches that because of sin nature is fallen into a situation that is hopeless unless something supernatural happens. The Christian mes-

1

sage is called good news precisely because it proclaims this intervention. God has broken into our world, and because he has, because there is saving power from outside of the natural realm, there is hope for those who look to him in faith.

Lewis wrote his book on miracles in 1947, a time when modernity was confident in its ability to derive truth "objectively" from science. Opponents of Christianity targeted their attack toward the miracles because, as Lewis agreed, if they could be disproved the entire biblical message would collapse. For this reason Lewis's book centered on a logical and biblical defense of the reality of miracles and the reasonableness of believing in them.

Lewis realized, however, that while his generation required a defense of the miracles themselves, there was a danger of missing the point of the miracles, that to which the miracles pointed. In the heart of his book, therefore, he presented a chapter titled "The Grand Miracle," by which he meant the coming of God's Son to the earth. This grand miracle provides meaning and purpose to all the other miracles in the Bible. Lewis writes:

> The central miracle asserted by Christians is the Incarnation. They say that God became Man. Every other miracle prepares for this, or exhibits this, or results from this. . . . There is no question in Christianity of arbitrary interferences just scattered about. It relates not a series of disconnected raids on Nature but the various steps of a strategically coherent invasion—an invasion which intends complete conquest and "occupation."[1]

This present book on the miracles of Jesus is written in a time that is in many respects quite different from Lewis's

SALVATION!

twentieth century. In his day the foes of Christianity were naturalists to the core; starting with the assumption that nature is all there is, they therefore declared the miracles impossible. There is little of that in our time. People today are open to the supernatural, indeed to supernatural forces of all kinds. The problem today is not that no one accepts the miraculous. Far from it! Our problem is that the miracles we believe are without any meaning or purpose outside of their individual benefits. They are "random acts of kindness" on the part of some benevolent but impersonal force in the universe.

In contrast, the miracles of the Bible, and especially in the Gospel narratives, are inherently purposeful. The miracles of the Bible have meaning because they are tied to that grand miracle of which Lewis spoke: the coming of Jesus Christ. Our chief purpose in studying the miracles of Jesus is to study him: his person and his coming and his work as Savior. The miracles provide us a clear lens through which to view that invading power that conquers and liberates, namely, the saving work of Jesus Christ our Lord.

The miracles speak powerfully about the person of Jesus Christ. Specifically they attest to his divine nature as God's Son. But the miracles provide their richest instruction regarding not just the person but also the work of Jesus Christ. And it is the work of Christ that saves us. It is not merely Jesus himself but what Jesus has done for us that we receive by faith in order to be saved. This is an important truth for us to realize, that we are not saved by our works but rather by receiving Jesus' work and its benefits by faith. In this important sense, we are saved by works—not our own, but the redeeming work of Jesus Christ. He alone is mighty to save.

It is Christ's saving work that his miracles so vividly reveal and manifest. The miracles were the companion to the great proclamation by which Jesus announced his coming: "The kingdom of God is near." As such, they provide a startling window into the whole message of salvation. In Jesus' miracles we encounter divine power for salvation, a mighty Savior and Champion able to defeat all the enemies that afflict and oppress us. Jesus' miracles serve as a foretaste and advertisement of his whole saving work. Through them we grasp the vast scope of his redemptive program, and we ground ourselves upon the rock of our hope and salvation, Christ's work for us as Savior.

A Prophet in His Hometown

The right place to begin our studies of Jesus' miracles is with his own introduction to the topic. All the Gospel writers mark the beginning of Jesus' public ministry at the Jordan River, where he received from John the Baptist the baptism of repentance. Overcoming John's objections, Jesus was baptized in fulfillment of Isaiah 53:12, which says he "was numbered with the transgressors." Jesus then was led by the Spirit into the wilderness, where he successfully overcame the devil's temptations (Luke 4:1–13). From the wilderness he returned to his hometown of Nazareth, there to announce the saving ministry he had earned the right to begin. There Jesus set forth the character of his messianic ministry.

In this opening chapter we will see his teaching and his works of power as they both declare Jesus' redemptive agenda. This passage, Luke 4:14–44, is rather long but forms a single literary unit. First we have Jesus' teaching in his hometown of Nazareth, which results in his rejection and an attempt to take his life. Then Jesus departs for Ca-

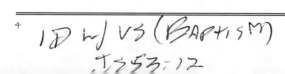

pernaum, where he performs two miracles and is happily received by a great many people. Luke's account begins with these words: "Jesus returned to Galilee in the power of the Spirit, and news about him spread through the whole countryside. He taught in their synagogues, and everyone praised him" (Luke 4:14–15).

This introduction tells us that when Jesus showed up in his hometown of Nazareth and entered into the synagogue on the Sabbath, the people had already heard of miracles he had performed in other nearby towns. We can only imagine how high the expectation ran, inspired by the reports that came before him.

This accounts for what happened in the synagogue. If what we know of later rabbinic custom held true in Jesus' day, as it likely did, the synagogue service began with a lengthy prayer, followed by a reading from the Torah (the five books of Moses) and then from the prophets, first in Hebrew and then translated into Aramaic. An eminent person would be asked to do the reading and to preach from the text.

What a scene it was, then, when Jesus was handed the scroll of the prophet Isaiah, to read and to speak—Jesus, the Son of God, the very Servant of the Lord written about by that ancient prophet but known to this audience mainly as a local son and now as the object of these amazing reports. It seems that Jesus was given liberty to pick his text. Luke tells us:

> The scroll of the prophet Isaiah was handed to him. Unrolling it, he found the place where it is written:
>
> "The Spirit of the Lord is on me,
>   because he has anointed me
>   to preach good news to the poor.

He has sent me to proclaim freedom for the prisoners
and recovery of sight for the blind,
to release the oppressed,
to proclaim the year of the Lord's favor."
(Luke 4:17–19)

This citation is mainly from the opening verses of Isaiah 61, although it also seems to contain a line from Isaiah
58. It is likely that Jesus would have had a number of chapters open to his eyes as he held up the scroll, and it would
not have been unusual for the reader to link together like
passages for the sake of one unified exposition. These lines
from Isaiah are particularly striking, not the least because in
them the voice of the promised Messiah, the Anointed
One, is heard speaking. We can imagine, I think, that the
voice Isaiah heard in his mind when receiving this
prophecy, the voice of God in revelation, was the voice
now heard in the synagogue at Nazareth. In applying these
verses to himself, Jesus was clearly defining his own calling
as that messianic ministry promised of old, for which Israel
had so long hungered and thirsted. The passage not only
identifies the speaker but also defines the character and
mission of his saving work.

Three key ideas are highlighted in this citation from
Isaiah. The first is that the speaker is the Anointed One
who bears the Spirit of God. "The Spirit of the Lord is on
me, because he has anointed me to preach good news to the
poor."

In the Old Testament, anyone set apart for a special
work might be anointed; all the kings of Israel, for instance,
were anointed by the pouring of oil. "Anointed One" is
what the term *Messiah* means, or *Christ* as it is in Greek.
And yet there was the expectation of one specially

anointed, the Servant of the Lord spoken about by Isaiah, the coming Messiah who would bring about the eschatological deliverance that would be the final salvation of Israel. Isaiah's first mention of the Servant began with this idea of divine anointing:

> Here is my servant, whom I uphold,
>   my chosen one in whom I delight;
> I will put my Spirit on him
>   and he will bring justice to the nations. (42:1)

When Jesus read these verses from Isaiah 61, his hearers would have thought of God's promised age of salvation for which they had been waiting.

That Spirit anointing had already occurred in the life of Jesus. His ministry was inaugurated by his baptism at the hands of John the Baptist, after which "the Holy Spirit descended on him in bodily form like a dove" (Luke 3:22) and the voice of God was heard commending him with words like those from Isaiah 42:1, "You are my Son, whom I love; with you I am well pleased."

Jesus was Spirit-anointed to fulfill two tasks, both of which are outlined in the rest of the quotation he reads. First, he was to be a prophetic witness to the good news of salvation. "He has anointed me to preach good news to the poor. He has sent me to proclaim freedom for the prisoners and recovery of sight for the blind." Jesus came to reveal the good news of what God had provided in him. Both John and Matthew refer to his coming as light shining in the darkness, the way of God and of salvation revealed to a world desperately in need of such revelation. It is to the poor that he comes, to those who are bound and who are blind. Luke's Gospel often emphasizes the social aspect of

salvation, and so he speaks of those poor in this world. Yet
there is a broader application here as well. He proclaims
good news to those who are poor in spirit, broken in heart,
those who mourn over sin and long to see spiritual light. To
them Christ came as the great and final prophet of the salvation to come.

There were many prophets who came before Jesus, Isaiah serving as an excellent example, as well as John the
Baptist. But what sets Jesus apart and above them all is the
second task for which he was anointed, that is, the accom-
plishment of the deliverance he proclaimed. God has sent
me, he says, "to release the oppressed." An ordinary
prophet could proclaim the promises of deliverance, but he
could not bring them to pass. John the Baptist had said,
"One more powerful than I will come, the thongs of whose
sandals I am not worthy to untie" (Luke 3:16). Here is the
One who comes not only with good news but also with
power to achieve what is promised—setting free those held
in captivity.

The final words of Jesus' quotation summarize his whole
mission and recall the jubilee year that was established under the Mosaic economy. He says he is anointed "to proclaim the year of the Lord's favor." In the jubilee year,
which came every fifty years, land was returned to its original owners and indentured slaves were set free. This all
pointed forward to that great day foretold by Isaiah:

> In the time of my favor I will answer you,
>   and in the day of salvation I will help you;
> I will keep you and will make you
>   to be a covenant for the people,
> to restore the land
>   and to reassign its desolate inheritances,

to say to the captives, "Come out,"
and to those in darkness, "Be free!" (49:8–9)

Such was the vastness of Jesus' claim that these verses
applied directly and specifically to him. He came as the
promised Messiah who would both reveal the salvation
from God and bring it to pass, with the result of freedom for
those held in bondage. Here was a figure like Moses, for Jesus' coming to Nazareth with these words was no less dramatic than Moses' appearance so long ago in Egypt, the
house of Israel's bondage. Indeed, Jesus is the greater One
to whom Moses had pointed (Deut. 18:18), the One who
would come not merely with news of deliverance but with
the power to break the chains that held God's people fast.

Jesus read the scroll and handed it back to the atten-
dant. With an evident intent to convey the dramatic, Luke
tells us "the eyes of everyone in the synagogue were fas-
tened on him, and he began" (Luke 4:20). The sermon that
followed was perhaps short, but it was unquestionably one
of the most profound ones ever preached. Jesus began with
these words, "Today this scripture is fulfilled in your hearing" (v. 21).

Two Responses to Jesus

In European villages, news of a victory in battle is received with the joyful clanging of church bells. In our own
time, news of a sports championship is greeted by thousands
of fans honking their car horns or racing into the streets to
cheer. The news Jesus was bringing was considerably more
important than these. What he proclaimed was nothing
short of Israel's hope of the ages. It was for this that thousands and thousands of priests had for years and years lit in-

cense in the Holy Place of the temple. It was for such news that generations of Jews had longed with a physical aching. And yet Alfred Edersheim is right when he describes the reaction in Nazareth as "an epitome of the history of Christ."[2] Here we have in microcosm what would be played out over the three years of Jesus' ministry. Edersheim cites John 1:11 (KJV) to describe the response: "He came unto his own, and his own received him not."

Luke provides a description that at least begins hopefully: "All spoke well of him and were amazed at the gracious words that came from his lips" (4:22). But by Jesus' reaction, it becomes clear that this was mere fascination; their real sentiment was expressed by the words that followed: " 'Isn't this Joseph's son?' they asked." The gist of it was this: "What are these words from a common man, one of us, as we know he is! We've seen him all his life, just Joseph's son!"

Knowing their mind, Jesus responded sharply: "Surely you will quote this proverb to me: 'Physician, heal yourself! Do here in your hometown what we have heard that you did in Capernaum' " (Luke 4:23). They wanted to see Jesus back up his claims with works of power, such as they had heard about from the nearby city of Capernaum. He should begin his healing at home, within his own circle, and until he did they would withhold their acceptance of his teaching.

Jesus did not give them the sign they were hoping for; as we will see, the miracles were never offered to charm the eyes of unbelief. Instead he replied, "I tell you the truth, no prophet is accepted in his hometown." He then gave them two examples from the Old Testament, examples that drove his listeners to madness (Luke 4:24–27), examples of a rejected grace that therefore went to others. The first was that of Elijah, who though rejected in Israel provided food during a famine to "a widow in Zarephath in the region of Sidon." The second example was Elisha cleansing only Naaman the Syrian of leprosy, while many lepers in Israel were left uncleansed. The point was not difficult to understand: God was willing to send his grace far from Israel because of their unbelief in rejecting his true messengers.

The clear implication was that Jesus was indeed a prophet and these his lifelong neighbors stood with those rebels of old who persecuted the prophets. Now was their chance to consider their attitude, to repent and believe, but the opposite happened. The furious listeners turned into a mob intent on punishing Jesus with death, thus rendering their verdict upon him. Luke tells us, "They got up, drove him out of the town, and took him to the brow of the hill on which the town was built, in order to throw him down the cliff. But he walked right through the crowd and went on his way" (4:29–30).

Thus Jesus of Nazareth walked out from the home of his youth, never, apparently, to set foot there again. Refusing to receive him in faith, the people of Nazareth would never see the miracles of power or receive the healings they had heard about from other places. Rejecting Jesus they had rejected the grace of God for salvation.

Jesus left Nazareth and made his way down to Capernaum by the sea, where again he taught in the synagogue and the people were amazed by the manner of his teaching. This time, however, a demon-possessed man called out to him by name, saying, "Have you come to destroy us? I know who you are—the Holy One of God!" (Luke 4:34). His hometown neighbors might not know Jesus, but the demons did. Jesus responded by rebuking the evil spirit, "Be quiet! Come out of him!" (v. 35). The demon obeyed, throwing the man to the ground, where he was found unharmed. Luke observes, "All the people were amazed and said to each other, 'What is this teaching? With authority and power he gives orders to evil spirits and they come out!' And the news about him spread throughout the surrounding area" (vv. 36–37).

Shortly thereafter Jesus went to the house of Simon Peter, whose mother-in-law was lying sick with a deadly fever. Jesus rebuked her fever, and she got up completely restored. Finally, before that same sun had set, multitudes with various ailments and demonic possessions came to Jesus, and a day that witnessed vast power from God ended with this outpouring of healing and restoration. You see what is so dramatically depicted by these events. What Nazareth had refused by rejecting Jesus now was outpoured in staggering abundance where faith was to be found.

The point is this: those who reject Jesus Christ reject the grace of God for salvation. But those who trust in him, who instead of driving him from their lives confess their need and bring all their ailments to him, receive a manifestation of saving power.

The Primacy of the Word

The goal of this first chapter is to understand what Jesus' miracles say about him and his work and how they bring his gospel into vivid light. Therefore we want to make general observations from what we have seen, the first of which is the relationship of the miracles to Jesus' teaching ministry. That relationship is one of subservience.

All through this passage Jesus' teaching is given the prominence. In the opening verses he is described foremost as a teacher: "He taught in their synagogues, and everyone

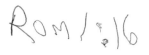

praised him" (Luke 4:15). Christianity is a faith and salvation driven by the power of a message, the gospel that is, as Paul put it, "the power of God for the salvation of everyone who believes" (Rom. 1:16). This is borne out in Isaiah's description of Jesus' messianic ministry, which Jesus read in Nazareth's synagogue. Three of the four verbs describing his mission have to do with teaching. He is to "preach good news," and twice he is told to "proclaim."

Of course, the prime example is Jesus' refusal to perform miracles unless the people first received his teaching. The Nazarenes wanted him to win their approval by a demonstration of power; we are reminded here of Satan's words in the desert, "If you are the Son of God, tell this stone to become bread" (Luke 4:3). Jesus refused the devil, and he refused the unbelievers in his hometown. "It is written," he said to Satan, " 'Man does not live on bread alone, but on every word that comes from the mouth of God' " (Matt. 4:4).

Even when Jesus went to Capernaum, it is interesting to note that both the exorcism and the healing of Peter's mother-in-law were achieved by Jesus' word. He rebuked the demon, and most strikingly, he also rebuked the fever. That seems odd. The same term is used in both cases—the Greek *epitimasen*—and in its fullest sense it indicates that he verbally subjected them to his authority. Later on Jesus would heal by a variety of means, but at the beginning he does so in a way that emphasizes the priority of his word.

In the same way, Christians and churches need an emphasis on the teaching of Christ, that is, the teaching of the whole Bible, above and beyond all subjective claims of spiritual power. Many people insist that teaching the Bible is insufficient for evangelism, church life, and Christian growth. They say that we must first set up signs and wonders or offer entertainment schemes to catch people's attention, to manipulate emotions to make people receptive to the Spirit's supposed working.

But that is not what we see in the ministry of Jesus Christ. Jesus did not use his miracles to attract interest, nor were they the focus of his ministry. His teaching was the focus, and we see this in what happened at the end of this passage. When the next day dawned and even greater masses thronged near for healing, Jesus pulled away from them and moved on. Luke 4:42 tells us, "The people were looking for him and when they came to where he was, they tried to keep him from leaving them." We can imagine the excitement of the disciples. Peter, with his typical worldly wisdom, would have seen a marvelous chance to grow a successful megachurch right there in Capernaum. "Imagine the opportunities!" Peter must have argued. "With your healing power we'll break all the synagogue attendance records. That'll show those fools in Nazareth!"

But Jesus did not think in such a manner. It was not that he lacked compassion or that he did not want to draw a vast multitude to his salvation. As history has shown, Jesus did intend to build a vast and mighty church. But he realized what we so quickly forget, that there can be no true salvation without the gospel and therefore without faith in his saving work. It was to preserve his teaching of the gospel from the worldly passions of the crowd that Jesus left. "He said, 'I must preach the good news of the kingdom of God to the other towns also, because that is why I was sent.' And he kept on preaching in the synagogues of Judea" (Luke 4:43–44).

Certainly we want to adorn the gospel with lives that manifest the grace of God, and surely we rejoice at his power that works in our midst. But if we want to follow Jesus' example, to employ the principles he showed in his ministry, then we will rely on the teaching of the Word of God, through which comes the power of God into this world as the gospel is received by faith.

A Divine Validation

The second thing to observe is that the miracles did provide a divine validation of Jesus' teaching. The miracles revealed his divine power even as they began the fulfillment of what he was preaching. Both of these miracles eminently demonstrate the very thing Jesus spoke of in the synagogue at Nazareth: "The Spirit of the Lord is upon me."

The author of the letter to the Hebrews looked back upon this when he was commending the gospel to his own readers. He wrote, "This salvation, which was first announced by the Lord, was confirmed to us by those who heard him. God also testified to it by signs, wonders and various miracles, and gifts of the Holy Spirit distributed according to his will" (Heb. 2:3–4).

Divine power testified to Jesus' divine message. Jesus cast out the demon, and the people responded with wonder: "What is this teaching? With authority and power he gives orders to evil spirits and they come out!" (Luke 4:36). It is often pointed out that Jesus did not teach in the manner of the scribes and Pharisees, relying on quotations from other religious leaders, but exposited the Scripture directly and with authority. But our passage emphasizes the effect the miracle had on his hearers. He taught the Word of God faithfully and with authority—that is primary—but then he demonstrated that authority in their midst, the miracle attesting to the divine character of his revelation.

In like manner, Luke's recording of the miracles served

to validate his Gospel to his original audience. He tells us, in the opening verses, that he carefully investigated accounts from eyewitnesses of what had taken place (Luke 1:2). Surely many of these people were still living; if these miracles could not be validated by those living witnesses, it would make a mockery of Luke's whole presentation. But the miracles did happen, Luke was not afraid of exposure, and this is a strong testimony to us of both the validity of these accounts and the supernatural character of Jesus and his teaching.

The miracles confront us with the same challenge they brought to that first-century audience: here is the Son of God, the divine Savior who rightly claims our allegiance. Darrell Bock puts it this way, speaking of the claims made by the miracles of Christ: "Jesus is no mere moralist. Neither is he merely a great motivator and psychologist. He is one with authority to defeat the evil forces that can dominate humanity."[3]

Jesus is the Savior from God, and his saving works performed so publicly oblige us to make a decision about him. That decision will define our relationship to the God who sent him, a decision to trust him unto salvation or to reject him as did the proud and stubborn people of Nazareth.

Victory and Healing

Third, and significantly, in this passage we see two aspects of Christ's saving work as they are revealed in salvation: his power, which wins victory, and his compassion, which bestows healing.

First we see his power, specifically as it relates to the overthrow of Satan and his reign in this world. It is noteworthy that the first miracle recorded by Luke is the casting out of a demon. Jesus came to undo the works of the devil. All his work was directed to rolling back the effects of the fall, our first parents' descent into sin and misery and death that was Satan's great achievement in this world. These saving works would culminate in Jesus' own death on a cross, and there Satan's power would be overthrown once and for all. The writer of Hebrews tells us this of Christ: "Since the children have flesh and blood, he too shared in their humanity so that by his death he might destroy him who holds the power of death—that is, the devil—and free those who all their lives were held in slavery by their fear of death" (Heb. 2:14–15).

We are going to look at demon possession in detail at a later time. But in light of Jesus' power over the demons that Luke sets before us, let me ask a question: Do you believe that there is power in this world capable of conquering the sin and darkness around you? It was Satan's work to bring sin into this world and therefore death and the curse of God on sin. Those tentacles have reached throughout human history, making a wreck of our race and leaving their mark on our own souls, a mark that many despair of ever removing. It is sin that holds us in chains—both our own sin, with the guilt and the corruption it has brought, and the sins of others by which we have been so deeply scarred and in many cases even emotionally or spiritually deformed.

This is what explains the state of this world around us. It is sin, and ultimately death, that holds us in slavery and fear. What or who can set us free? Here is the answer: Jesus Christ came into the world to undo the works of the devil, to roll back the reign of sin and death. Especially his death on the cross accomplished what Charles Wesley so memorably described in his great hymn:

He breaks the power of reigning sin,
He sets the prisoner free;
His blood can make the foulest clean,
His blood availed for me.

The casting out of demons was but a foretaste of his great work at Calvary, as well as a preview of what is yet to come—the expulsion of Satan and all his works from God's new creation, the resurrection kingdom. This is what Jesus ultimately heralded: "The kingdom of God is near!" (Mark 1:15). His coming proclaims and guarantees that the reign of darkness is broken. He strikes down our enemy, and, as Isaiah had written, he sets the captives free.

That is one side of Jesus' work of deliverance, a glorious foretaste and a promise of Satan's final overthrow. The healing of Peter's mother-in-law shows us a second aspect of his ministry, namely, Christ's compassion for all who receive him as Savior and Lord.

Simon Peter believed Jesus enough to bring him home, where his mother-in-law lay ailing. Luke says, "They asked Jesus to help her" (4:38). With great compassion he responded, overcoming the ailment that subjected her. When word got out, others came, and people with all kinds of sickness were brought, and Jesus took notice of them all. Luke says, "Laying hands on each one, he healed them" (4:40). He released them from demons and from the affliction of sickness and disease, each one receiving attentive grace from the heavenly Physician.

What is this but a great invitation for people to come to Jesus with their weakness and their sickness of body and soul, to race to him who is able and willing to help and to heal, to save and restore? "Come to me," he cries out into the ages. "Come to me, all you who are weary and bur-

dened, and I will give you rest" (Matt. 11:28). His coming
brings the year of the Lord's favor.

> [He comes] to preach good news to the poor
> . . . to bind up the brokenhearted,
> to proclaim freedom for the captives
> and release from darkness for the prisoners.
> (Isa. 61:1–2)

Strength for the Weak, Riches for the Poor

That brings us to the fourth and final point about the
meaning of the miracles. Jesus' miracles are directed not to
the rich but to the poor, not to the strong but to the weak,
not to the proud of heart but to the humble and the broken
in spirit. John Calvin rightly points out the implication of
what we see in this passage: "The only way we may enjoy
these benefits of Christ, is to be humbled by a serious real-
ization of our ills, and to seek for Him as hungry men seek
their liberator. Those that are full of pride, and do not
groan in their bondage, find no discomfort in their blindness, despise this oracle with deaf ears."[4]

Isn't that right? Isn't that what happened in Nazareth?
They were focused on their rights, their demands, their
claims to merit. But the only way to come to Christ is the
way the hymnist described:

> Out of my bondage, sorrow and night,
> Jesus, I come, Jesus, I come. . . .
> Out of my shameful failure and loss,
> Jesus, I come, Jesus, I come. . . .
> Out of unrest and arrogant pride,
> Jesus, I come, Jesus, I come. . . .

Out of the fear and dread of the tomb,
Jesus, I come, Jesus, I come. . . .

The only way we can come to Jesus for salvation is to face and own our guilt, our sin, our weakness and spiritual bankruptcy. But look at the power, look at the compassion, look at the riches with which he saves the poor and the lost! Therefore do not delay, do not refuse, for as the people of Nazareth learned, the opportunity may not come again. This is what the apostle Paul wrote about years later when he shared the concern of every servant of the gospel:

We urge you not to receive God's grace in vain. For he says,

"In the time of my favor I heard you,
and in the day of salvation I helped you."

I tell you, now is the time of God's favor, now is the day of salvation. (2 Cor. 6:1–2)

And so it is. This too is the meaning of the miracles of Jesus. Do not delay, do not refuse Jesus Christ, do not forfeit salvation out of pride or ignorance of your true situation. Come to him who wields the message and the power of deliverance, come as one poor, as one sick and needy and blind to the light of heaven, and by the power that is in Jesus Christ, you will be saved.

2

"I Am Willing"

Luke 5:12–16

*When he saw Jesus, he fell with his face to the ground and
begged him, "Lord, if you are willing, you can make me
clean." Jesus reached out his hand and touched the man.
"I am willing," he said. "Be clean!" And immediately
the leprosy left him. (LUKE 5:12–13)*

In our study of the miracles of Jesus Christ we are working
from the premise that we have before us something more
than random acts of kindness. These miracles are not
merely illustrations of Christ's goodness and power but are
living sermons regarding the nature and purpose of his sav‐
ing work. We might say that the text the miracles expound
is that great prophetic statement of anticipation found in
Isaiah 63:1, where the prophet asked, "Who is this, robed
in splendor, striding forward in the greatness of his

strength?" The Lord replied, "It is I, speaking in righteousness, mighty to save."

Jesus began his ministry teaching and healing and calling disciples to himself. Early in the Gospels we see a high
concentration of miracles, as Jesus eagerly went about the
work he had announced from the synagogue in Nazareth:
"To proclaim freedom for the prisoners and recovery of
sight for the blind, to release the oppressed, to proclaim the
year of the Lord's favor" (Luke 4:18–19). In Luke 5 we encounter a particularly vivid portrait of his saving power as
Jesus confronts the dreadful sight of a man stricken with
leprosy.

The People Jesus Saves

If the miracles set forth the full scope of redemption,
they also speak volumes about the objects of Christ's saving
work. How are we to describe those whom Christ saves?
This passage gives us a telling description. Luke tells us,
"While Jesus was in one of the towns, a man came along
who was covered with leprosy" (5:12).

The Bible's term *leprosy* describes a broad range of skin
diseases and does not always correspond with what we
know by the name of Hansen's disease. Included in the biblical term are psoriasis, lupus, ringworm, and favus.
Nonetheless the first thing we must say about leprosy in the
ancient world is that *it was a horrible condition*. Particularly
in its advanced stages it was debilitating and terribly disfiguring. It affected not merely the surface of the skin, with
sores and splotches, but also corrupted the blood and rotted
the bones. To have leprosy was to be ravaged in body
through and through, a living death.

Perhaps more dreadful than the disease itself were the

social and religious implications of being a leper. According to the law, as set forth in Leviticus 13–14, a leper was banished from all human contact, removed from the family and the workplace, from the synagogue and the market, cast outside the city to live in shadows. Consider Leviticus 13:45–46, which commanded: "The person with such an infectious disease must wear torn clothes, let his hair be unkempt, cover the lower part of his face and cry out, 'Unclean! Unclean!' As long as he has the infection he remains unclean. He must live alone; he must live outside the camp."

One reason for these restrictions was the risk of contagion. But it is also clear that leprosy represented sin and its corruption. Lepers were physically impure, but more importantly they were ceremonially impure, unclean, and thus shut off from the ordinances of salvation. Indeed, we read in the Old Testament of leprosy sometimes occurring as a result of divine punishment, as in the cases of Moses' sister, Miriam; Elisha's wayward servant, Gehazi; and King Uzziah when he transgressed the temple precincts.

To be a leper was horrible. Surely this man felt it keenly, which is what brought him to Jesus. Mercifully, he had no mirror to gaze into and see his wretched face. But he could see his hands with the horrid white splotches. He could feel the aching in his bones. He heard the cries of horror whenever he approached other people, as when now he drew near to Jesus; he saw the gasps of shock when people set their eyes on him, and he felt the pain of loneliness when they ran away.

Of course, this leper represents every person in the bondage and corruption of sin. His unclean skin signifies the work of sin upon us, the fruit of our own evil deeds and the sins of others as they have impacted us. His rotten bones signify the corruption of sin that is within us. As the leper is the living dead, so too are we "dead in transgressions and sins," as the apostle Paul remarks (Eph. 2:1). Like leprosy, sin is debilitating; it cripples our lives and relationships and our every work. It is disfiguring, marring not merely our expressions but also the image of God with which we were made. The leper's alienation speaks of the true fellowship and love that eludes us because of sin and most pointedly to our alienation from God.

At least this poor leper saw his horrid condition, and therefore he ventured to come to Jesus. How few of us see the truth of our leprous condition. And yet there is ample, if not equal, testimony. How can we look at our hands and fail to see the splotches from the evil they have done? Do we not look into our hearts and feel the aching of sin's corruption? How can we deny the cravings of a sinful nature, the delight in what is lewd and perverse, the ugly and malicious thoughts like foul blood running through our veins?

Many of us do not feel unclean because we have never committed adultery or murder, because our lies have been petty ones, because though we have stolen we have never been caught. Some look to human standards and see other people doing the very things they are doing, and therefore they don't feel unclean. But if our conscience fails to show us the horror of our condition, God provides a mirror with which we can see ourselves truly. That mirror is his law, most central of which are the Ten Commandments. There we see the perfection of God's character and of his divine standards. In that mirror we discover stains upon our face. We see an impotence within ourselves. We see that we are cursed and diseased and unclean. Perhaps this is why Matthew, in his Gospel, put the story of this leper after the

Sermon on the Mount, where Jesus pressed a true understanding of the law upon his listeners:

> You have heard that it was said to the people long ago, "Do not murder, and anyone who murders will be subject to judgment." But I tell you that anyone who is angry with his brother will be subject to judgment. . . .
> You have heard that it was said, "Do not commit adultery." But I tell you that anyone who looks at a woman lustfully has already committed adultery with her in his heart. (Matt. 5:21–22, 27–28)

You see that the leper does represent us, horrible and unclean with the scars and the corruption of iniquity.

This leper was not only horrible, but also *his case was hopeless.* Rarely, and only if they were caught early, some of the minor conditions described as leprosy might be cleansed. But Luke tells us that this man was "full of leprosy," and so his case was hopeless. Society had written him off and hoped only to see him no more. All that awaited him was misery followed by death—a description people are using more and more to describe life in the leper colony that is this world. Misery, followed by death.

This leper knew himself to be hopeless, except that Jesus might save him. But I wonder if you do. You have seen this description of sin, and you recognize some acquaintance with yourself, but you will seek improvement, you will make resolutions, you will turn a new leaf. But do you realize that the reason you do the things you do is that you like them? It is your nature that is corrupt, your nature that inclines to self-worship, to self-satisfaction at the expense of others. You may succeed, I admit, at some surface improvements. You may scrub a splotch or two off your skin. But realize that they will only reappear, since the problem is the disease that afflicts you, that resides within you, and for which there is no earthly cure.

The leper saw that he was horrible and hopeless, and thus he ventured to come to Jesus. So too must we.

Encouragement to Come to Jesus

What an encouragement it is to us that this man came to the Lord Jesus Christ, for if he can come so can we. Charles Haddon Spurgeon noted three reasons this leper may have had to stay away but which we do not have.

First, his coming to Jesus was *without precedent*. Up to this point, the Lord had healed many sick people, those afflicted with fevers and similar ailments. He had cast out demons. But the horror of a man filled with leprosy, a man barred even from setting foot in the city, was completely without precedent. Perhaps he had heard that in the synagogue of Nazareth Jesus mentioned the Syrian leper healed by Elisha and so was encouraged to come. But we have a far greater encouragement, for Jesus has healed many people like us. Before us runs a veritable highway of the greedy and the promiscuous, the angry and those in despair. Every Christian church is filled with those who have slain with the tongue, lovers of iniquity, and worshipers at the feet of idols, who yet have come to Jesus Christ for cleansing and salvation.

Second, this leper had *no promises*. We do not read of Jesus seeking out lepers, crying out for lepers to come for healing—except that he came to seek and save all who are lost. And yet the leper came, crying, "Lord, if you are willing, you can make me clean." We, however, cannot plead the excuse of lacking promises, even great promises that pertain precisely to our condition. Consider these wonderful words from the prophet Isaiah:

> Let the wicked forsake his way
>   and the evil man his thoughts.
> Let him turn to the LORD, and he will have mercy
>   on him,
>   and to our God, for he will freely pardon. (55:7)

Finally, the leper came with no invitation, but we have been called and invited by Jesus himself. Our Lord stood before all the world crying: "Come to me, all you who are weary and burdened, and I will give you rest. Take my yoke upon you and learn from me, for I am gentle and humble in heart, and you will find rest for your souls" (Matt. 11:28–29).

Indeed, with his last words in the Bible, the final cry of the risen and exalted Lord Jesus, he calls from heaven for us: "The Spirit and the bride say, 'Come!' And let him who hears say, 'Come!' Whoever is thirsty, let him come; and whoever wishes, let him take the free gift of the water of life" (Rev. 22:17).

The Leper's Faith

Why, with all that against him, did the leper come? He came because he saw the enormity of his need, and then he came because he saw Jesus. Look at what Luke tells us about what he did and said: "When he saw Jesus, he fell with his face to the ground and begged him, 'Lord, if you are willing, you can make me clean'" (5:12).

It is clear that if nothing else the man recognized the deity of Jesus. Coming to Jesus, he prostrated himself in the position of worship and pleaded, addressing Jesus as Lord. Given the culture of the Orient, all of this might have been done merely as an expression of deference and respect, with no implication of deity. But that cannot be said about these words, coming from a man afflicted with leprosy: "You can make me clean."

We think back to the case in the Old Testament of Naaman the Syrian. Naaman was a high-ranking general who learned from his Israelite slave girl about a prophet in Israel who could cure him of the leprosy from which he suffered. He went to his own king, who sent a letter to the king of Israel asking that he arrange for his general to be healed, offering a large sum of money in return. The Book of Second Kings tells us what happened: "As soon as the king of Israel read the letter, he tore his robes and said, 'Am I God? Can I kill and bring back to life? Why does this fellow send someone to me to be cured of his leprosy? See how he is trying to pick a quarrel with me!'" (2 Kings 5:7).

So it was well known in the ancient world that even a king could do nothing about a man covered with leprosy. At a minimum, this leper came to Jesus believing that he was a great prophet, like Elisha, bearing some divine power to heal and to save. That is the first thing we see about his faith—he identified Jesus as one bearing divine power for salvation, indeed the only Savior for his condition.

And yet there was some internal struggle at work within this leper. He did not merely say, "I know you can make me clean." Instead, he said, "Lord, if you are willing, you can make me clean." He knew that Jesus had the power, but he was not sure that Jesus was willing to use it in his case. He knew Jesus was a Savior, but he was not convinced Jesus was willing to save him.

We can well imagine this poor leper looking on as Jesus came down the road. Perhaps he had witnessed Jesus healing others; perhaps he had heard Christ's teaching about the kingdom of God and realized that this was the Savior. But then he argued with himself. "I see he is able. But is he willing? Everyone else shuns me and shrieks at my approach. Will he? My condition is one of shame, strongly associated with sin and God's curse. Will Jesus reprove me, when he has received others? I am horrible to behold, cast out by the law of God itself. Will Jesus be willing to make me clean, though surely he is able?"

How many people feel this way! They see well enough that Jesus is the world's only Savior. But is he willing to be their Savior? They note that Jesus loves the children, but they have long since lost their childlike innocence. They see him commending those who serve God, but they have given their talents mostly to themselves. They see his penetrating gaze working behind the façade to see the things that are so shameful. Surely, if he is God, he knows the words they have spoken in bitterness, the blasphemies that have rolled off their tongue. Is he willing to take them now? He knows what beds they have lain in and what things their hands have grasped after. "He is able, but is he willing for such as me?"

Surely that is the kind of debate that raged within this leper's heart. It seems that he came to Jesus without fully resolving the issue. Instead, he fell down before the One who alone was able to heal him and begged, "Lord, if you are willing, you can make me clean." He placed the matter in Jesus' hands, and that is what we must do as well.

"I Am Willing"

How beautiful was Jesus' reply, plain and direct: "I am willing." Why was Jesus willing to make this wretched man clean? Mark, in his account of this miracle, gives us one answer. He says Jesus was "filled with compassion" (Mark 1:41). What a statement, in light of what is said of this leper. He is full of impurity, full of uncleanness, full of leprosy, so he doubts there is anyone willing to help him. But Jesus is full of compassion, so that he is willing. His compassion corresponds to the level of the leper's corruption: he is full of it. He came into this world to know us in our sufferings, to feel the pang of thirst and the weariness of the flesh. He came and suffered temptation himself, and therefore he is able, even as God, to sympathize with our suffering and our trials. Jesus is willing to save you, not because of what is in you, not because you are lovely or lovable, but because of what is in him. He is "filled with compassion." And that is the first reason he is willing.

We see the other reason Jesus is willing in his response to the leper. Luke 5:13 wonderfully tells us, "Jesus reached out his hand and touched the man. 'I am willing,' he said. 'Be clean!' And immediately the leprosy left him."

I think the touch of Jesus' hand was astonishing to this leper. He believed that Jesus could make him clean, but he did not dream that Jesus could touch him. He dared to hope this healer would cure him, but he dared not hope Jesus would place his warm, human hands upon his wretched skin. The crowds parted as he came near; others who were waiting for Jesus fled to come back some other day, for there was a leper in their midst. But notice Jesus did not first cleanse him and then touch him; he touched the one who was unclean, in his unclean state. And then, only then, did Jesus say, "Be clean."

What does this say about Jesus' attitude toward you, in the reality of your impure heart, your unclean body and spirit? This means that he is willing, willing to reach into whatever garbage heap you are to be found, willing to reach through the sewage that clings to your soul, willing to touch you as you are, in order to have fellowship with you, as Savior and as Lord.

There are many people of whom our world is sick and tired, whose stench nobody wants to smell anymore. They have used up all the benevolence of their family and former friends, no longer deemed worthy of hope or help or even of prayer. Like this leper they are the living dead. Do you know someone like that? Is that someone you once cared for—or perhaps even you?

Then look at this scene of our Lord Jesus touching the leper in his uncleanness. Here is the second reason he is willing: he can reach into death because his is the power of life. "In him was life," wrote the apostle John, "and that life was the light of men" (John 1:4). He is light, and so he can touch the darkness. He is pure, and so he can touch the unclean. The leper does not defile Jesus, as even a brush of the skin would do for any other man; instead the touch of Jesus purifies that which is unclean.

Worthy of our interest are John Calvin's reflections here:

> There is such purity in Christ he absorbs all uncleanness and pollution, He does not contaminate Himself by touching the leper, nor does He transgress the Law. . . . [He] stays whole, clears all our dirt away, and pours upon us His own holiness. Now, while He could heal the leper by His word alone,

He adds the contact of His hand, to show His feeling of compassion: no wonder, since He willed to put on our flesh in order that He might cleanse us from all our sins. . . . Here is a thing which we pass over without much impression at an idle reading, but must certainly ponder, with much awe, when we take it properly—that the Son of God, so far from abhorring contact with the leper, actually stretched out His hand to touch his uncleanness.[1]

Immediately, miraculously, the leper was clean and whole. Jesus was willing, because of his great compassion and because he is able to save us to the uttermost, by the power of God that is in him.

Be Clean!

What this means is that there is cleansing for you, no matter how horrid the scars upon your heart, no matter how wretched the stench from your soul, no matter how unclean and defiled and impure you are. Jesus said to the man who was filled with leprous uncleanness, " 'Be clean!' And immediately the leprosy left him." What a picture this is of the total and instantaneous cleansing that is available for sinners who come to Jesus. Because of this God is able to say, "I will forgive their wickedness and will remember their sins no more" (Heb. 8:12). Therefore the psalmist can sing, "As far as the east is from the west, so far has he removed our transgressions from us" (Ps. 103:12).

Jesus' power to cleanse is not true in only a judicial way, that is, in terms of our standing before God—though that itself is wonderful and necessary good news. It was also of great concern to Jesus that this man be restored to fellowship with God's people and returned to the ordinances of God—in short, that the leper be reconciled to God. That is why he insisted, in Luke 5:14, "Go, show yourself to the priest and offer the sacrifices that Moses commanded for your cleansing, as a testimony to them."

But Jesus not only took away the stigma of uncleanness, the curse of leprosy. He made the leper clean. Let me then ask this: Do we believe Jesus can do that for us? Do we believe that he can touch the places of our shame, our degradation, our uncleanness, and do what he did for this leper? "Be clean!" he said, and the man was clean.

When we come to Jesus he makes us clean. People come to him defiled in sexual sin, and he gives them the heart and the purity of a virgin. Others still are coarse, are braggarts, are gossips. Christ brings forth sweet fountains from their lips, a blessing to people and a pleasure to God. If we will come to him, he will make us clean. If we ask he surely will say, "I will. Be clean!" He invites us to bring before him whatever it is that stains our heart and burdens our soul, to bring it to him who is willing and is able. Spurgeon says it so well when he writes, "The 'I will' of an emperor may have great power over his dominions; but the 'I will' of Christ drives death and hell before him, conquers disease, removes despair, and floods the world with mercy. The Lord's 'I will' can put away your leprosy of sin, and make you perfectly whole."[2]

No Other Name

The miracles of our Lord set before us the vast scope of his redemptive work. What does this passage show us but that Jesus came to a world of men and women filled with uncleanness? Horrible and hopelessly defiled. This is what his saving work accomplishes when he applies it to sinners, like his hand reaching out to touch the leper's skin—he takes away not merely the stain and the curse of our sin but also the corruption of sin itself. This tells you who have never called out to Jesus for salvation that you can. Indeed, you must—or you will never be healed of your leprous corruption. As the apostle Peter said in Acts 4:12, "Salvation is found in no one else, for there is no other name under heaven given to men by which we must be saved."

Even if you deny your wretched state there is a day coming that will bring everything to light. There is no reason to go on deluding others and yourself, when God has made a way for you. The apostle Paul tells us this: "You see, at just the right time, when we were still powerless, Christ died for the ungodly. . . . God demonstrates his own love for us in this: While we were still sinners, Christ died for us" (Rom. 5:6–8).

Therefore there is no reason to withhold your shame, your filth, your fears from him who came as the Great Healer, even of lepers like us. You may only find grace to say, "Lord, I don't know if you are willing in a case so foul as mine. But I know that you can, and I come to you for cleansing." Will he not say to you what he delighted to say to this poor leper? "I am willing. Be clean!" As the apostle John assures us, "If we confess our sins, he is faithful and just and will forgive us our sins and purify us from all unrighteousness" (1 John 1:9). And may he then find glory for himself in our hearts, as we respond with thanks and praise to him.

WHICH IS MORE IMPORTANT

3

Authority to Forgive

Luke 5:17–26

_"Which is easier: to say, 'Your sins are forgiven,'
or to say, 'Get up and walk'? But that you may know that
the Son of Man has authority on earth to forgive sins....'
He said to the paralyzed man, "I tell you, get up,
take your mat and go home." (LUKE 5:23–24)_

Many of the miracle accounts contain a great many details.
The danger this poses is becoming overly fixated on these
details while missing the important point that is being
made. This third miracle account is like that. There are a
great many people involved: Jesus, the paralytic, the four
men who brought him to Jesus, and the teachers of the law
who opposed our Lord. Not only are there many people but
also there is a great deal of activity. There is the persistence
of the four men, which results in the dramatic lowering of

the lame man through the roof. There is Jesus seeing their faith and then seeing the accusations taking place in the hearts of the teachers, both of which show his divine faculties in action. There is Jesus' remarkable response to the lame man's faith. Then there is the doubt of the teachers of the law, followed by Jesus' response to them, his dramatic healing of the paralytic as a sign of his authority, and finally the amazement of them all as the man who had been lame went home praising God.

That is a lot to consider in one study, and yet there is a clear meaning to it all. The story points us to the forgiveness of sins that is the focus of Jesus' ministry. In this chapter we see this come to bear in three ways: the purpose of Jesus' ministry, which is the forgiving of sins; the authority Jesus has to grant the forgiveness of sin; and the faith in Jesus that is the only way for sinners to receive forgiveness of their sins.

The Man on the Mat

The recipient of this miracle was a man who suffered from paralysis. He was unable to stand up or walk, and so his friends brought him to Jesus on a stretcher.

We have observed in our studies of the miracles that these people we read about are not random individuals to whom Jesus showed kindness. The miracles represent Christ's saving work, and correspondingly, the people he heals portray the human race in need of salvation. This lame man, lying helpless, unable to walk, therefore is a picture of humanity in sin.

Let me get at this by citing a phrase that is often used to disparage religion in general and Christianity in particular. Sometimes you will hear it said, "Christianity is a crutch for the weak." This is a travesty against the Christian faith, and I am always offended when I hear it. But the reason for my offense is not that it goes too far. The problem is it doesn't go far enough! Christianity is not a crutch for the weak. People on crutches are getting along, albeit a bit slowly. If they wait a bit things will normally get better. That is not what Christianity is. Christianity is a resurrection for the dead, sight for the blind. It is the lame and crippled and helpless man coming to Jesus Christ and hearing the words, "Take up your mat and walk!"

What this man represents is spiritual inability and deformity. People take offense at this kind of teaching. But let me point out that we just celebrated the end of a century that began with unprecedented confidence in human ability and goodness and strength. "Man is getting better every day, in every way"—that actually was the motto a century ago. Go back and read the magazines and books; you will see their clear confidence in human ability, their basic optimism about what humanity was going to do in the years ahead. They had great hopes for leaving poverty and war and misery far behind, and yet we have progressed no further than a man paralyzed and lying on a mat. The century that was to see the end of war has been the bloodiest on record. While material riches have grown, we are yet surrounded by impoverished lives on every side. Suicide, drugs, crime, and abuse all bear testimony to a societal misery that cannot be ignored or explained away.

Humankind is not moving forward and never will except as men and women are brought before Jesus Christ like this paralytic. That is why the apostle Paul characterized people apart from Christ as "without hope and without God in the world" (Eph. 2:12). As we burst upon a new millennium it is really the same old world we have always known. The issues today are not new; we have not moved beyond the concerns of a year ago or a generation ago or a millennium ago. The real problems are not how to land machines on Mars or how to explore the genetic code. D. Martyn Lloyd-Jones put it this way:

> The problems are: what is life; how can a man live in a decent manner; how can a man control himself and his impatience and his baser instincts and desires; how can a man live as a man; how can he so live that even if he is stricken down by an illness, or shattered by an accident and loses everything on which he has depended, he is still all right; how can a man sing in a prison? These are the questions. How can a man die? They have always been the questions, they are still the same; there are no new problems.[1]

Today's issues are really yesterday's issues dressed up in new clothes. On our own there is no hope of overcoming them. As far as transcending or solving these great problems, humankind has made no more progress than a paralytic lying on a mat.

What is true for society as a whole is also true of us as individuals. Our basic selfishness, for example, does not change but merely manifests itself in different circumstances and phases of life. The same may be said for our handling of death. We may one day ignore it, another day cringe before it, and another lash out in anger and despair. But we do not conquer death, nor can we ultimately avoid it, try though we might. Like this man on the mat, none of us is able to get up and walk out of the human condition, the human predicament in sin, and the human helplessness in the face of death. A. W. Tozer was right when he observed, "The soul of man does not change fundamentally, no matter how external conditions may change. The aborigine in his hut, the college professor in his study, the truck driver in the bedlam of city traffic all have the same basic need: to be rid of their sins, to obtain eternal life, and to be brought into communion with God."[2]

Carried by Four

The paralytic in our story does move, however, carried by four friends who deliver him to Jesus. Luke tells us, "Some men came carrying a paralytic on a mat and tried to take him into the house to lay him before Jesus. When they could not find a way to do this because of the crowd, they went up on the roof and lowered him on his mat through the tiles into the middle of the crowd, right in front of Jesus" (5:18–19).

What a great example this is of a Christian ministry. These four men understood what the paralytic needed: he needed to come to Jesus Christ. They were determined that they were going to get their friend to the Savior. Would that we had such determination with our friends and neighbors and family members!

Think of these four men. They might have stayed in the house, listening to Jesus teach on and on. And who would have faulted them for that? But they thought of their stricken friend who could not come, and they went out for him. "Go, make disciples," Jesus commanded us. And we will have to go out and get them like these four did.

We can imagine them addressing this paralyzed man and telling him of Jesus who possessed power to heal. He might have said, "I am willing to go, but you will have to get me there." That is true for us as well. We may desire an old friend or a brother or a sister to come to Christ, because we know full well he is the only One who can heal them. But we will have to get them there. We will have to pray diligently for God to move their heart. We will have to set an example that will give credibility to our words. We will have to listen to and answer their worldly objections and hardhearted evasions. It may take four of us for any one of them. It may take a mother who prays for years, along with a teacher who shows patience and care, plus a colleague at work who seems different from other people and who candidly speaks of salvation in Christ. Then there will be a neighbor who shares an extra Bible and takes him along to church, and "overnight" he is converted. That is how evangelism works. Think of how you came to Christ, how many factors were combined, how many hands there were on the stretcher that brought you to the Savior.

That is what the Christian ministry is all about. We are not merely advocating a lifestyle or particular family values. We are bringing men and women to Jesus Christ. That is where the healing power is. We are not trainers of certain spiritual techniques or a club taking in new members. Rather, we are emissaries of the Lord Jesus Christ, disciples and disciple makers, and ours are to be the hands that take hold of the lame and bring them to the church, to the preaching of the gospel, to Jesus Christ who is the Savior of the lost.

Of course, these four men had an obstacle to overcome, namely, the massive crowd that blocked the way to Jesus. Most of us would have said, "Well, it must not be the Lord's will for this man today." "If the Lord had wanted him to be saved, then he would have cleared the street." But that is not what they said. They were inventive and persistent, and they are an excellent example for us of the creativity and determination of which the gospel is worthy.

Jesus was teaching in a typical house. It probably had one story inside with its second story outside in the open air, so the roof would have been accessible by outside stairs. These men estimated where Jesus was, and they began digging their way through. Before long they had removed the thatch and pulled aside the tiles, and then they did the one thing they could do—they lowered their friend down right in front of Jesus. They could not go in; they would not be there to tell either the man or Jesus what to do. None of that mattered, for they had gotten the sick man to the Great Healer, and he would do the rest.

"Your Sins Are Forgiven"

Here we have one of those great tension-filled moments we so often see in the life of Jesus. We can easily imagine the scene. There in the room is Jesus, surrounded by a throng of people, many of whom have come with hopes of being healed, others straining for a word of grace, still others doubting and evaluating everything he says. As Jesus is speaking, the sounds of men on the roof are heard, and then an opening is made and this paralytic is lowered down at his feet. Surely there was stillness in the room as all perceived the tension. What is this? What will Jesus do? Will he heal him? Will he rebuke them? Perhaps there were several moments of such silence, with this man lying at the feet of the Lord.

Jesus was delighted by what he saw, and we are told why. Luke 5:20 says, "He saw their faith." How can you *see* faith? We might say that Jesus saw their hands as they plowed through the roof, he saw the determined looks on their faces as the four let him down, he saw the look of hope and belief that dawned on the paralytic's face when finally he rested before the Savior. We might then ask ourselves, "How do people see my faith? What are the visible signs of my trust in Jesus Christ?"

But there is more to it than that, because the Bible says that Jesus saw their faith. Jesus saw the signs of faith, but he who reads the hearts of men saw their faith itself. He sees the faith of those who can hardly see it themselves. How often when we are discouraged by sin or wracked by doubt, Jesus sees our faith. And so, as the prophet says, "A bruised reed he will not break, and a smoldering wick he will not snuff out" (Isa. 42:3). Jesus responds to a faith that he sees, and so in response to this man's faith he now spoke.

Breaking the silence, looking down upon the man with compassion, Jesus declared, "Friend, your sins are forgiven." What an amazing response to the man's faith! Here he is at Jesus' feet in obvious need of a cure, and Jesus says not, "You are healed," but "Your sins are forgiven."

A good number of the commentators conclude that Jesus obviously said this because the cause of this man's paralysis was some particular sin. Saying "Your sins are forgiven" was his way of healing this man's psychosomatic ailment. But that is a poor reading of what is happening. We are brought in the story to a point of tension—four men interrupting Jesus' teaching to lower a lame man in through the roof. There Jesus is with the intruder now before him and the crowd waiting in anticipation for what Jesus will do. And what does he do? He takes advantage of the dramatic scene to heighten and then to capture their attention and ours.

As Luke relates the story, we are expected to be surprised by Jesus' words: "Friend, your sins are forgiven." But it was not just Luke's telling of the story; this was the way it happened. What we are seeing is the way Jesus employed the opportunity, the drama, and the tension to focus the crowd on the great issue for which he came—not just the healing of bodily sickness, but the healing of spiritual corruption, even the forgiveness of sins.

Some of the commentators point out that there is a link between spiritual health and bodily health, and that is true. But to focus on this is to miss the point. Yes, Jesus linked this man's paralysis to sins, that is a clear and significant point, but not in a simple cause-and-effect relationship. The greater point is that sin is at the root of all the brokenness of this fallen world. Death entered into the human condition with Adam's first sin, and when Jesus sees the effects of the fall—when he sees leprosy or paralysis or loneliness or broken hearts—it is sin that he thinks of.

One of the better recent commentators, Donald Hagner, explains the main link between sin and sickness:

> In the biblical view, all sickness and suffering, like death itself, traces back to the entry of sin into the world. In this sense all sickness is caused by sin. . . . The point of this narrative is that the problem of sin, though not as apparent to the eye as paralysis, is a fundamental—indeed . . . [it is] the fundamental problem of humanity that Jesus has come to counteract. Compared to the healings, the forgiveness of sins is by far the greater gift Jesus has brought in his ministry.[3]

There is something important here to be aware of. What is the problem of this world? Is it that basically good people are placed in bad environments? Is it that ignorance and narrow traditions have chained us in darkness and we lack a proper and enlightened education? Is the problem that bad people have seized the reins of power and imposed a perverse set of laws upon the nation?

Here is the point, and it is a vital one, because how we conceive of the problem of this world determines what kind of solution, what kind of salvation, is required. If the problem is a bad environment, the solution is social engineering. If the problem is ignorance, then education is our only hope. If bad laws are the enemy, then legislative action is the way of salvation.

We have lately concluded a century that sought salvation down all of these routes, and may I suggest that the results call for some reconsideration? Decades of social engineering in this country have done little more than display the vanity of human wisdom. Education has not unlocked a new tomorrow; indeed, our universities are more the scenes of despair than of enlightenment. What about legislation? It is good to have just laws, but the problem with our country is not merely the laws but the grip sin has upon us as a people.

When Jesus said to this man, "Your sins are forgiven," he was pointing to a different and deeper problem than these. Man is alienated from his God, he is held captive by sin, and from it he cannot get up and walk away. He is held back by the guilt of sin, so that a chasm spans between him and God. He is crippled by the power of sin, so he cannot walk in paths of righteousness, regardless of what laws are passed or what environments we concoct.

All of this explains why Jesus acted as he did. He dealt first with the core issue of sin before addressing himself to the symptoms, such as this man's paralyzed condition.

When Christ was born, he was named Jesus because, as

the angel had said, "He will save his people from their sins" (Matt. 1:21). John the Baptist identified Jesus at the beginning of his public ministry by saying, "Look, the Lamb of God, who takes away the sin of the world!" (John 1:29). He had in mind Christ's sacrificial death on the cross, where he would carry the sins of all those who trust in him. Later Peter would write, "He himself bore our sins in his body on the tree, so that we might die to sins and live for righteousness; by his wounds you have been healed" (1 Peter 2:24).

Forgiveness of sin is the healing Jesus had in mind when he came into the world. And with all the crowds clamoring around him for healing of their bodies, Jesus used this choice opportunity, as the paralytic lay before him, to point out the true purpose of his ministry—the forgiveness of sins for all who look to him in faith.

Faith in Christ brings many blessings. It will, for instance, produce better environments, it will make you a better student, it will lead to justice and civic peace. Fellowship with God inevitably leads to wholeness all through our lives. But we should never place any of these above or before the forgiveness of our sins. That is the first and greatest blessing, and it ought ever to be the principal source of our thanksgiving.

But how many Christians grumble against God, bemoaning the things they have not received, things they think they should have, acting as if God has let them down? And yet the status from which they rail against him is that of pardoned criminals. They come, hungry orphans adopted into a lavish home, protesting that the fare is not up to their high standards.

When our sins have been forgiven, we should never complain to God or accuse him when lesser gifts have been withheld. God's gifts are governed by his wise and good and

sovereign purpose. We may suffer, we may lose spouses or never have them, we may be poor or lame or persecuted. But all these, with forgiveness of sins, mean that we have life eternal, fellowship with God as beloved children, and true spiritual blessings that will last forever. But without forgiveness, nothing else can bring real or lasting blessing. If I possess all my fondest dreams but remain an unpardoned sinner, then I have nothing. Jesus taught, "What good is it for a man to gain the whole world, and yet lose or forfeit his very self?" (Luke 9:25).

Authority on Earth

That is the first point we must see: Jesus' central purpose in the forgiveness of sins. But this raises a second issue, one that was keenly felt by some in the crowd: Does Jesus have the authority to grant such forgiveness? That is an issue we need to be sure about as well.

In 5:17 Luke informs us, "Pharisees and teachers of the law, who had come from every village of Galilee and from Judea and Jerusalem, were sitting there." That is quite an audience. Rising sports stars today will have an arena filled with scouts and recruiters. Aspiring singers dream of record company executives watching from the audience. This was Jesus' chance to impress this entourage of Pharisees, except that he was not courting their approval.

This is the first appearance of the Pharisees in Luke's Gospel, and they get off to quite a bad start. They had come to sit in judgment on Jesus, to check out what he would say and do, and then to seize upon any problems. How Jesus obliged them when he pronounced the forgiveness of the paralytic's sins! We read their thoughts in Luke 5:21: "Who is this fellow who speaks blasphemy? Who can forgive sins but God alone?"

What these teachers of the law specialized in was not so much the Bible but the oral tradition passed down from rabbi to rabbi. Jesus would attack this tradition all through his ministry as the teaching of man that leads people away from God. Ultimately these men would arrange Jesus' death on this very charge of blasphemy, the offense they ascertained in his words of forgiveness, since forgiveness is God's alone to grant.

On the surface there is reason to sympathize with the Pharisees. After all, Jesus' words were exceedingly bold. Jesus was taking up an authority that I, for instance, do not have. If I see evidence of faith in someone I may well console him or her with assurances of pardon from God's Word. But I can hardly read the heart of a man I have just met and who has not yet even spoken, and then declare with authority, "Your sins are forgiven." But, of course, neither can I say what Jesus went on to say, "Take up your mat and walk." There was the proof of his authority to forgive. Here is what happened:

> Jesus knew what they were thinking and asked, "Why are you thinking these things in your hearts? Which is easier: to say, 'Your sins are forgiven,' or to say, 'Get up and walk'? But that you may know that the Son of Man has authority on earth to forgive sins. . . ." He said to the paralyzed man, "I tell you, get up, take your mat and go home." (Luke 5:22–24)

We need to picture how strongly Jesus was confronting those who doubted and opposed him. They haven't even had the chance to verbalize any objection before he tells them exactly what is on their minds. And then he refutes them with this amazing miracle. "No one can forgive sins," they were thinking, "except God alone." And Jesus responds with this striking demonstration of divine authority such as they had never seen before.

Does Jesus have authority on the earth? Is his forgiveness of sins a valid one? That is a question we need to be sure about. Jesus answered the doubts by an astonishing miracle of healing. But, we might reason, there are others who claim to be able to heal. The apostles healed and they were not God, although they claimed to do such miracles only on behalf of and in the power of Jesus. False prophets may claim to perform healings, even to arrange false shows of power. Jesus warned us about false Christs (Matt. 24:24), and we are told in the Bible that Satan has power that might be used in miraculous displays (2 Cor. 11:14).

This last matter is an important one because the Pharisees would ultimately accuse Jesus of wielding satanic power in his miracles. Jesus retorted that the character of his whole ministry was heavenly and not hellish; those who could mistake Jesus Christ for the devil have written their own condemnation.

What Jesus claims here—divine authority to forgive—is validated all through this Gospel and then sealed at the end of his life. Ultimately it is on the cross that his claim to divinity is upheld. It was there as he died, as he gave himself for the healing of the world, that the centurion and his guards saw the darkness at midday, they felt the earth tremble, they heard Jesus crying out to his Father, and they concluded, "Surely he was the Son of God." Then at the open tomb, when he was raised from the dead, God gave public testimony before all history that this Jesus was his beloved, accepted Son. It is on public record for the world to behold.

Jesus has authority to forgive sins because of his own divine status, but most importantly because he bore in his own body all the sins he forgave people like this paralytic, people who look to him in faith. As the apostle Peter would write, "Christ died for sins once for all, the righteous for the unrighteous, to bring you to God" (1 Peter 3:18). Ultimately that is why Christ has authority to forgive. J. Gresham Machen puts it this way: "Jesus is our Saviour, not by virtue of what He said, not even by virtue of what He was, but by what He did, He is our Saviour, not because He has inspired us to live the same kind of life that He lived, but because He took upon Himself the dreadful guilt of our sins and bore it instead of us on the cross."[4]

Faith on the Mat

Jesus came to bring forgiveness of sins. As God's Son and as the One who bears them on the cross, he has authority to grant that forgiveness. There remains one thing for us to discuss, and that is the manner in which men and women receive that forgiveness. The answer is found in this passage, in the contrast between the two kinds of people and the response Jesus makes to each of them.

There were the Pharisees, who doubted and accused Jesus, who came not because of their sense of need but rather proud of themselves and their cause. They came not seeking forgiveness but rendering judgment. They came as those who were well, not as those in need of a physician; as the proud and not the humble; as the just seeking credit rather than the guilty seeking forgiveness.

It was not the Pharisees who received forgiveness then, and it is not people like them who are forgiven today. Rather, it was the poor, broken man who looked to Jesus in faith, carried by his believing friends. What did he do? He came to Jesus in his weakness, in the grip of sin, and he trusted him for salvation. That is what you and I must do as well. The apostle Paul writes, "In him we have redemption through his blood, the forgiveness of sins, in accordance with the riches of God's grace" (Eph. 1:7).

In Christ is where we must place our faith. John adds in his first epistle: "If we claim to be without sin, we deceive ourselves and the truth is not in us. If we confess our sins, he is faithful and just and will forgive us our sins and purify us from all unrighteousness" (1 John 1:8–9). That is what we must do: confess our sin and ask Jesus for forgiveness. God does not require us to perform religious services, the kind the Pharisees loved. He does not require us to pay him money or to fulfill some romantic quest. No, he demands that we confess that there is nothing we can do to earn salvation, then confess our guilt to him and come to Jesus like this man on the mat.

When you do that you will receive everything from him, by his grace and to his glory. You will hear him say to you, "Friend, your sins are forgiven." After that, he will tell you to pick up whatever mat you are lying on and walk in newness of life. When you do that, and when he does his promised work of grace, you too will go forth praising God, even as the watching world marvels at what God has done for you.

4

"Just Say the Word"

Luke 7:1–10

*He was not far from the house when the centurion sent
friends to say to him: "Lord, don't trouble yourself, for I do not
deserve to have you come under my roof. That is why I did
not even consider myself worthy to come to you. But say the
word, and my servant will be healed. For I myself am a man
under authority, with soldiers under me. I tell this one, 'Go,'
and he goes; and that one, 'Come,' and he comes. I say to
my servant, 'Do this,' and he does it." (LUKE 7:6–8)*

Our studies of the miracles of Jesus Christ have focused
mainly on three elements. First there is the sickness or
other desperate condition that creates the need for Jesus'
intervention. Luke, who we remember was a physician,
often gives considerable detail in this respect, and we have
had occasion to observe how well these sad figures portray

humanity's plight in sin. The second element is the faith of the person who comes to Jesus, and finally there is Jesus, who shows his readiness to save by healing the person in view.

This passage from Luke 7 departs from that pattern somewhat, primarily in that Luke tells us very little about the man who needs to be healed. In fact, he does not appear but is simply described. The emphasis is on the astounding faith of the Roman centurion, as well as on Jesus' delight in finding this kind of fervent belief.

The story begins with Jesus returning to Capernaum, having given what in Luke is known as the Sermon on the Plain, which corresponds to the Sermon on the Mount in Matthew's Gospel. As he returns, Jesus is approached by a delegation of Jewish elders who ask him to look favorably upon an unusual request from a centurion in the Roman garrison. Luke tells us, "A centurion's servant, whom his master valued highly, was sick and about to die. The centurion heard of Jesus and sent some elders of the Jews to him, asking him to come and heal his servant. When they came to Jesus, they pleaded earnestly with him, 'This man deserves to have you do this, because he loves our nation and has built our synagogue' " (7:2–5).

With little comment, Jesus left with them toward the centurion's home. As they approached, the centurion sent a second delegation, a group of friends who relayed this message:

> "Lord, don't trouble yourself, for I do not deserve to have you come under my roof. That is why I did not even consider myself worthy to come to you. But say the word, and my servant will be healed. For I myself am a man under authority, with soldiers under

me. I tell this one, 'Go,' and he goes; and that one, 'Come,' and he comes. I say to my servant, 'Do this,' and he does it." (Luke 7:6–8)

Our Lord's response to this amazing encounter was twofold. First, he turned to the crowd following him and said, "I tell you, I have not found such great faith even in Israel" (Luke 7:9). Second, he healed the servant, for we read in verse 10: "Then the men who had been sent returned to the house and found the servant well."

In this chapter we will focus first on the centurion and his lowly self-esteem; second, on this great faith that Jesus so highly praises; and finally, on this excellent portrait of Jesus in his office as Savior.

The Lowly Centurion

As we examine the interesting figure that is this Roman centurion, we find that he poorly represents the ideals of our own therapeutic age. I say this because far from showing the importance of high self-esteem he commends the opposite. This soldier is an amazing example of a lowly self-esteem, and he shows the value of such humility for the Christian faith. Particularly astounding about this man's humble demeanor are the many natural reasons he had for thinking quite the opposite about himself. I can see five such reasons that are readily evident.

First, this man had considerable authority over others. A centurion was a middle-ranking Roman officer, in charge of about one hundred soldiers. While he had little power outside of those affairs entrusted to him, within his sphere he had absolute dominion. He makes this clear in Luke 7:8: "I tell this one, 'Go,' and he goes; and that one, 'Come,' and

he comes. I say to my servant, 'Do this,' and he does it."
Very often that kind of power leads one to think himself superior, to dwell on what gives him such a right. Furthermore, most midlevel officers are trying to claw their way up
the chain while fending off the ambitions of those below,
neither of which lends itself to humility.

Second, this centurion *was part of an occupying army.* He
and his soldiers were in the role of conquerors, subjugators of
a defeated people. This too tends toward high-mindedness.
Obviously, such people calculate, there is a reason why they
hold sway over such distant nations. We don't know that
this centurion was Roman; it is certain that he was at least
a Gentile in the employ of Herod Antipas, the local Roman
puppet, who was allowed to raise his own legions. If you
take these first two reasons together, it would have been
natural for him to have approached Jesus quite differently
than he did. He might have summoned Jesus bluntly, or-
dering him to do him this service as his natural right. But
instead we see this great humility. The centurion seeks the
intercession of a group of friendly Jewish elders, meekly en-
treating Jesus for help.

The favor of these elders might well be another reason for
a high view of himself. It is not easy for us to receive praise,
the way this centurion does, without it going to our heads.
With every layer of brick added to the synagogue this centurion paid to build, his self-righteousness might well have
risen higher. The Jewish elders would have collaborated in
this high view of himself. "This man deserves to have you
do this," they said to Jesus, "because he loves our nation
and has built our synagogue." How marvelous, then, it is to
see his self-appraisal: "Lord, don't trouble yourself, for I do
not deserve to have you come under my roof."

Furthermore, the centurion *was a fairly wealthy man.* By

current standards, centurions were paid enormously well, and he had money to spread around. Adding to this was a fifth reason, namely, his competence that is implied by his rank. A centurion in the Roman army needed to be an accomplished soldier, leader, and administrator. None of these, however, led him into the kind of pride that so often makes a ruin of souls.

I mention all these reasons because most of you have at least one of them for an erroneously high view of yourself. You have money or status, good works, ability, or people who praise you. If it comes to it, you are able to find inferiors around to look down your nose upon.

There is nothing wrong with the kind of self-respect that appreciates things of value and worth. In that sense we speak of taking pride in our work or our community or our family. Christian parents should not be afraid to tell their children they are proud of them, although they will want to take care to stifle the impulse to self-glory. But the pride that despises, the pride that boasts in self, the pride that demands of others and worst of all demands from God—that we must avoid on the peril of our souls. C. S. Lewis poignantly described the great evil there is in self-glorying pride:

> The essential vice, the utmost evil, is Pride. Unchastity, anger, greed, drunkenness, and all that, are mere fleabites in comparison: it was through Pride that the devil became the devil. Pride leads to every other vice: Pride is the complete anti-God state of mind . . . Pride is spiritual cancer: it eats up the very possibility of love, or contentment, or even common sense.[1]

This centurion successfully avoided all this, as his entreaty to our Lord Jesus shows. It was through his humility that he was blessed, and his example is a great encouragement to us. In particular, I want to point out three great benefits he gained from his low view of self.

The first benefit of humility is that it brings us into correspondence with the true state of affairs. The centurion said to Jesus, "I am unworthy," and those were not empty words. The Scripture teaches, "There is no one righteous, not even one. . . . All have turned away, they have together become worthless; there is no one who does good, not even one" (Rom. 3:10, 12). Again, "There is no difference, for all have sinned and fall short of the glory of God" (Rom. 3:22–23). Though we think highly of ourselves, God reminds us, "Dust you are and to dust you will return" (Gen. 3:19). Or, as the prophet writes,

> All men are like grass,
>   and all their glory is like the flowers of the field. . . .
> The grass withers and the flowers fall,
>   but the word of our God stands forever
>   (Isa. 40:6, 8)

All this being the case, it is good for us to be lowly in our self-esteem in order to see things as they are.

The second benefit of this centurion's humility is seen in his dealings with others. It is worth our attention that he who was so humble was also so kind. We see the tenderness of his affection for his servant, which must have been rare for that time. We also see his kindness toward the Jews, who were, after all, the people he was there to dominate with raw force. The proud are never kind or gentle, but this Roman centurion—a man whose life was built on rugged strength—had learned how to love with gentleness and meekness because of his humility of heart.

Third, and this is what is most important, the centurion's humility put him in the right place before God. A lowly self-esteem is the prerequisite for rightly dealing with the Lord of heaven. As the apostle Peter reminds us, "God opposes the proud but gives grace to the humble" (1 Peter 5:5). Humility puts us in the place where God delights to bring blessing. It unstops our ears to the gospel by magnifying our sense of need. Humility is essential for any true and godly spirituality. The Scriptures have always emphasized this, as we read in Isaiah 57:15,

> For this is what the high and lofty One says—
>   he who lives forever, whose name is holy:
> "I live in a high and holy place,
>   but also with him who is contrite and lowly in
>   spirit,
> to revive the spirit of the lowly
>   and to revive the heart of the contrite."

Lowliness of heart, comprehension of our sin, dread of God's austere holiness, and agreement with our sentence of condemnation—all of these commend the gospel, the cross of our Lord Jesus Christ that we then see as the only salvation for our souls. Godly humility alone opens our mouths to speak, with the apostle Paul, "May I never boast except in the cross of our Lord Jesus Christ" (Gal. 6:14). A. W. Tozer sums up its value with these words:

> True humility is a healthy thing. The humble man accepts the truth about himself. He believes that in his fallen nature dwells no good thing. He acknowledges that apart from God he is nothing, has nothing, knows nothing and can do nothing. But this

knowledge does not discourage him, for he knows also that in Christ he is somebody. He knows that he is dearer to God than the apple of His eye and that he can do all things through Christ who strengthens him.[2]

This centurion may not have yet arrived at all of this understanding, but his lowly self-esteem was a good beginning, opening the door to the riches of faith in Christ.

Great Faith in Israel

Thus it was that when Jesus drew near to the centurion's house, he hastened to send a second delegation. "Lord, don't trouble yourself, for I do not deserve to have you come under my roof. That is why I did not even consider myself worthy to come to you" (Luke 7:6–7). It is probably true that this gesture was motivated not only by humility but also a concern for Jesus based on an awareness of the Jewish law. He knew that the house of a Gentile was no place for a rabbi, and he put Jesus' interests before his own.

That must have impressed our Lord. But what the centurion said next caused Jesus to beam with joy: "Say the word, and my servant will be healed. For I myself am a man under authority, with soldiers under me. I tell this one, 'Go,' and he goes; and that one, 'Come,' and he comes. I say to my servant, 'Do this,' and he does it" (Luke 7:7–8). Jesus marveled at these words, and he turned to those who were following after and remarked, "I tell you, I have not found such great faith even in Israel" (v. 9).

What a remarkable statement that is. Sadly, Jesus had encountered much unbelief and opposition among the people of Israel. We think back to his hometown of Nazareth, where those who once were his neighbors rejected him and tried to drive him over a cliff. We think of the scribes and Pharisees who had scorned him when he spoke of the forgiveness of sins.

But there were others who did show faith in him. There were the disciples, like Peter, who brought him to heal his mother-in-law. There was the man covered with leprosy, who believed Jesus could heal him, even if he doubted that Jesus would. Up to this point, the greatest example of faith in Israel was that shown by the four men who had lowered the paralytic through the roof, certain of the healing that was to be found in Jesus.

But here, in the most unlikely of places, in a Gentile and a military officer as well, Jesus finds greater faith yet than he has seen in any son of Israel. The centurion believed that Jesus could and would heal his beloved servant. We have seen the depth of his faith in the humility of his demeanor; in contrast to the Jewish elders he did not claim his merit but his unworthiness. We see also the reverence with which he treats the Lord. He obviously perceives Christ's excellence and the divine office he bears. In Luke 7:6 the centurion addresses Jesus as Lord, which is more than the Jewish elders did. All of this must have contributed to Jesus' appreciation.

But obviously it is in the comparison he makes that Jesus finds so much to praise: "Say the word, and my servant will be healed. For I myself am a man under authority, with soldiers under me" (Luke 7:7).

The whole point of this comparison is that the centurion exercises authority that he receives from his superior. The Roman military system was built on iron discipline, and this discipline was rooted in the principle that centurions and other officers wielded power that came from the emperor. To disobey a centurion was to disobey the emperor; as a result absolute obedience was the norm. "I am a man under authority," he said, "with soldiers under me." The point therefore is clear: Jesus too has received authority from the One above him, an authority that gives him authority not merely over a certain number of men but over sickness and death itself, an authority which therefore is of God. As R. C. Sproul observes, "Here was a man who had stood before generals, maybe even the emperor of Rome, who knew somehow that in Christ he was dealing with One who exercised consummate lordship."[3]

No wonder that Jesus marveled at this extraordinary perception. Sproul goes on to observe:

> He had not been born and raised in the shadow of the synagogue, he had not been steeped in the literature of the Old Testament, he had not known intimately the oracles of God found in the prophets. . . . But he understood authority and he understood that Jesus had it. He understood that Jesus had a kind of authority that gave him the ability to have power over life and death. . . . He understood the thing that escaped the religious leaders of Jesus' day; the obvious manifestation of God incarnate, which took place in the midst of people that were blind to it, was recognized by a Gentile.[4]

Understanding that Jesus was the One sent from God with authority over life and death and sickness, in a way analogous to his own authority over Roman soldiers, the centurion merely asked that Jesus say the word. "Just say the word and it will be done, for yours is the power. Just will it to be so, for space and distance are no barrier to you; at your command my servant will be healed." So it was, for when the messengers returned to the centurion's house they found his servant healed, and no doubt they found the centurion rejoicing over what Jesus had done.

A Study of the Savior

Surely we think highly of this centurion who thought little of himself and much of Jesus. Jesus marveled at his faith, which sets an example for us. But the One who ought to fill us with wonder is not the centurion but Jesus himself.

The portrait of Jesus in this passage is an especially precious one, boldly presenting him in his office as Savior. The first thing we notice is his willingness to go. We might think lightly of this until we consider the barriers that might have caused him to do otherwise.

The first of these is the poor recommendation from the Jewish elders. "He deserves to have you do this," they assured Jesus. That may be the way we commend people to one another, but that is no way to commend someone to God. We have already seen that God opposes the proud but exalts the humble. God insists on being sovereign in salvation; he saves by grace and by grace alone. He says, "I will have mercy on whom I have mercy, and I will have compassion on whom I have compassion" (Rom. 9:15). Later in the Gospels we encounter the rich young ruler who came to Jesus on the merits of his own law keeping. To him Jesus replied, "No one is good—except God alone" (Luke 18:19), and sent him away to learn humility before God.

But Jesus saw through the petty words of these elders and perceived the faith of him who sent them, unwilling to come himself, unwilling as a Gentile to approach Jesus without intercession from the Jews.

That brings up another barrier, and it was not a small one. Jesus was a Jew, under the law, and this centurion was a Gentile. According to the law, Jesus could not go into the centurion's house without defiling himself. The centurion seems to have been acutely aware of this problem, but to Jesus it was no barrier. Jesus is the One who fulfills the law, who is described by the law; therefore anyone he sees fit to bless is made clean by him.

With the coming of Jesus Christ, the boundary lines of this world have been radically redrawn. Before Jesus it was circumcision that marked the boundaries of the people of God. But the promises to Israel were fulfilled in the coming of Jesus; indeed, he is the recipient of all that they hoped for, and in him their inheritance is available to everyone. Alfred Edersheim comments, "Jesus shares with Abraham, Isaac and Jacob the fulfillment of the promise made to their faith. Thus we have here the widest Jewish universalism, the true interpretation of Israel's hope."[5]

For that reason this man's status as a Gentile was no barrier to Jesus Christ. This great reality is set forth more clearly in Matthew's Gospel, which is thought to have been written to Jewish believers and yet most strikingly emphasizes the true universalism in Christianity, which is the true Israel of faith. Matthew tells us these additional words Jesus said on this occasion:

> I tell you the truth, I have not found anyone in Israel with such great faith. I say to you that many will come from the east and the west, and will take their places at the feast with Abraham, Isaac and Jacob in the kingdom of heaven. But the subjects of the kingdom will be thrown outside, into the darkness, where there will be weeping and gnashing of teeth. (8:10–12)

Those words must have stunned Jesus' Jewish hearers, because it turned against them all that their externalized religion had come to represent. It is not the circumcision of the flesh that counts but the circumcised heart that believes on Jesus Christ—of such are the people of God. From the east and the west, all sorts of cast-outs and left-behinds, those who come into saving relationship with God through Jesus Christ, shall feast at his banquet while those who reject him, regardless even of their status as Jews according to the flesh, are left outside (see Matt. 22:8–10).

One thing this means is that there is hope for you. Whatever barrier there is between you and God is no barrier to the Savior Jesus Christ. Perhaps your sins testify against you, that you cannot belong to God. But Jesus overcomes your sins; voluntarily he died to bear the guilt of all who trust in him. What about your status in the world? Are you one who has been far from God, far from his church? Learn that his power traverses all distances in response to faith. He breaks down every barrier to bring together a new people united in him. The apostle Paul wrote about people perhaps like you: "Now in Christ Jesus you who once were far away have been brought near through the blood of Christ. For he himself is our peace. . . . Consequently, you are no longer foreigners and aliens, but fellow citizens with God's people and members of God's household" (Eph. 2:13–14, 19).

Jesus is willing—that much is clear from the beginning of this account—but this passage also makes clear that *he is able to save* everyone who trusts in him, regardless of their conditions or the circumstances.

If we stand back and observe all that Jesus does in this account, what an encouragement we have of his power to save! Consider the situation. Jesus is told of a man he has never seen, who is sick and about to die. Matthew tells us the man was paralyzed and suffering horribly. Without the slightest hesitation, without a moment's reflection about the momentous task ahead of him, Jesus went with them. Charles Haddon Spurgeon therefore observes, "It shows, dear friends, our Lord's conscious ability to deal with all manner of evil, since he was not at all puzzled by this intricate case. . . . Though the case perplexed many, it did not perplex the Lord Jesus, for he said, 'I will come and heal him.' "[6]

That being the case, we should never despair for ourselves or for others. If we trust in him, we will ourselves hear the blessed words of our Savior: "I will come and heal."

Finally, we gain a glimpse at the heart of our Lord Jesus, as well as his sense of priorities, even his own sense of wonder. Jesus marveled at this faith. We might ask, What was Jesus looking for as he set down that road with the works-righteous Jewish elders? If all he was interested in was a miracle, he need not have gone anywhere, for his simple word sufficed. Nor would he then have stopped short but would have proceeded to the centurion's house if it was a healing he marveled to see. But it is no extraordinary thing to Jesus that the Son of God has power to heal. This is commonplace to him, however hard it is for us to absorb. No, we have to say that *what Jesus went looking for was faith*; encountering this great faith he marveled in his heart. This is what brought him such special joy.

How much better if we were more like Jesus, not craning our necks for extraordinary phenomena, not craving signs and wonders that are impressive to the flesh, but seeking humble faith that magnifies and honors the Lord. This is the wonder of this world, the thing that makes angels sing and God rejoice. Would that we were more like the apostle Paul, who wrote in the introduction of his letter to the Colossians, "We always thank God, the Father of our Lord Jesus Christ, when we pray for you, because we have heard of your faith in Christ Jesus and of the love you have for all the saints" (1:3–4).

Eyes on Jesus

This centurion's faith sets a worthy example for us. Surely he had inquired of doctors and received their hopeless reports. But he did not fix his gaze on the patient but upon the Great Physician that is Jesus Christ. He did not limit his hopes by the powers available on this earth but sought him who brings power from heaven to save and to heal, trusting Jesus' simple word for his need.

The reality is that if we had more faith we would see far better results. If we looked not on the extent of people's unbelief and love of sin but on Christ's saving power, we would be far bolder in our witness about him. If we formed our thoughts not on what the world can do to us but on what God can do in us and through us, we would fear very little in the way of intimidation or threat or temptation. If we believed more in the simple power of God's Word to transform lives, we would pray more earnestly for his blessing on the Word in our church, in our own lives, and in the lives of those we would boldly invite to come and hear the Word of the Savior. Most importantly, if we saw half his power to save we would never fear to come to him for all our own needs, and especially for the forgiveness of our sin.

He is strong; therefore let us not be put off by our weakness. Let none despair for lack of resources, but rather let us take heart from his omnipotence. What we lack he has. He says, "My grace is sufficient for you, for my power is made perfect in weakness" (2 Cor. 12:9).

As this centurion observed, the Son of God has authority from heaven to save, authority to heal, authority to protect and to lead us and to keep us and to save us to the uttermost. Let us then fix our eyes on Jesus, calling upon him for our every need, and not only will he deliver us but also he will delight in the heart that trusts in him. "Such faith!" he will say. "It is what I have been looking for!"

5

Weep No More

Luke 7:11–17

When the Lord saw her, his heart went out to her and he said, "Don't cry." Then he went up and touched the coffin, and those carrying it stood still. He said, "Young man, I say to you, get up!" The dead man sat up and began to talk, and Jesus gave him back to his mother. (Luke 7:13–15)

The Bible contains a great many wonderful promises. In John 6, Jesus declares, "I am the bread of life. He who comes to me will never go hungry, and he who believes in me will never be thirsty" (v. 35). In John 8 he described himself as the "light of the world" and promised, "Whoever follows me will never walk in darkness, but will have the light of life" (v. 12). Matthew 11 contains a famous promise. Jesus calls out to the weak and weary, "Come to me, and I will give you rest" (v. 28). Matthew's Gospel ends with another great promise: "Surely I am with you always, to the very end of the age" (28:20).

The most comprehensive promise of all comes in the seventh chapter of the Book of Revelation. There the angel shows the apostle John the great multitude of the saints in heaven, from every nation and every tribe, wearing white robes and holding palm branches as they worship in the presence of God and of the Lamb. The angel told John that the redeemed are before God's throne day and night, and then he made this great statement: "Never again will they hunger; never again will they thirst. The sun will not beat upon them, nor any scorching heat. For the Lamb at the center of the throne will be their shepherd; he will lead them to springs of living water. And God will wipe away every tear from their eyes" (vv. 16–17).

The miracles of Jesus are closely related to God's promises in the Scripture. Indeed, they give us previews of coming attractions. They offer a foretaste of all that will be when the promises are fulfilled. These individual miracles point to a far more comprehensive miracle. They are particular deliverances and salvations that deal with particular people and situations, and yet they speak of a greater deliverance, a greater salvation that is available to all through the gospel.

This passage from Luke 7 is like that. It is a brief account, with just a few words and actions. But here unfolds a great miracle that points to a comprehensive salvation for all who sorrow and struggle and look to Jesus for comfort. "Weep no more," Jesus said to the mourning widow. And at his touch and mighty call the son who was dead came back to life. Where once was only sadness, suddenly there was great joy and praise to God. That is what this miracle account shows us: first, Christ's compassion at the scene of desolation; second, his power of life that reigns over death; and finally, the awe and wonder of those who stood by watching, overflowing into praise to God.

The Widow in Tears

One thing you will notice if you study the Bible is that there is a great deal of weeping going on. If you trace words like "crying" and "wept," you will find yourself also tracing the history of God's people. With few exceptions all the major figures of the Bible are seen weeping, and in all sorts of situations. There is Abraham broken in mourning over the dead body of his wife, Sarah (Gen. 23), and Esau crying in frustration after his brother, Jacob, had stolen the covenant blessing of his father (Gen. 27). When Joseph was elevated from slavery to great power in Egypt and then his brothers arrived seeking aid, he wept over the years that had been lost and the fellowship that had been broken (Gen. 42).

Jephthah's daughter, sentenced to death by her father's foolish vow, roamed the hills, weeping over the wedding she would never have (Judg. 11). Naomi cried with Ruth and Orpah at the cruel parting brought on by their widow-hood (Ruth 1:9), and Hannah wept quietly in the house of the Lord over the barrenness of her womb (1 Sam. 1).

In the story of David there is as much weeping as there is rejoicing. We see him and his beloved friend Jonathan embracing and crying when young David had to flee for his life (1 Sam. 20). Years later tears flowed down David's face as he sang a funeral dirge for Jonathan, who had fallen in battle with his father, wicked King Saul (2 Sam. 1). When David was king he wept over the discovery of his own evil deeds in the affair with Bathsheba and Uriah (Ps. 51). Later still, bitter tears filled his eyes when one son died in infancy (2 Sam. 12) and another, Absalom, died in rebellion against David (2 Sam. 18).

King Hezekiah cried in sickness and pain and fear for his life (2 Kings 20). Jeremiah, the weeping prophet, lamented the fall of rebellious Jerusalem. By the waters of Babylon, the people of God wept in memory of Zion (Ps. 137). And when Zerubbabel led the return and the rebuilding of the second temple, the older priests who had seen the original in all its glory wept aloud while younger men shouted for joy (Ezra 3:12).

Peter the disciple of Jesus wept bitterly, we are told, when the rooster crowed and he realized he had betrayed his Master three times. And the shortest verse in the Bible tells us of Jesus standing before the sealed tomb of his dead friend, Lazarus: "Jesus wept" (John 11:35).

Somewhere in that survey are tears you too have shed. You either have wept in mourning or in frustration or in repentance or in fear, and if not, you will before too long. That being the case, these words from Jesus' mouth, "Weep no more," are words for you.

Of all the sad figures in the Bible, however, few rival the woman in this brief story. She was a widow, and her only son lay dead in an open coffin as she led the procession out the gates of Nain, a town some forty kilometers southwest of Capernaum. Luke tells us there was a large crowd going with her, and their loud wails fit the picture of this desolate woman. Her despair would have had several facets. First, no doubt, was the emotional side to this disaster. We are not told details about her situation, but surely it was a blow to her when her husband had been taken down this very road to be buried. Undoubtedly she would then have leaned upon their son for her comfort. He would have reminded her of her husband; she would have smiled to see aspects of his character coming out in the young man. But now, with this death, as she walked this bitter trail once more, the blow was redoubled, and she must have mourned terribly.

There would be an economic side to this tragedy as well. Unless she was quite wealthy, widowhood would mean great financial straits. Now, with her only son gone, she might be facing desperate times. Finally, there would have been a spiritual side. There would be no descendant to carry her name forward until the coming of the Messiah; she was cut off from the future of her people. How easy it would be for her to see in all of this God's curse upon her, the disfavor of heaven for some vengeful or even capricious purpose. No doubt others would come to that conclusion, and when the time of mourning was over their pity might turn to contempt and disdain.

It is interesting to note that the widow of Nain is one of three outcast figures that appear in the seventh chapter of Luke's Gospel. According to the standards of that time, these three would qualify as the figures most disenfranchised, most abandoned by God, and the furthest from his grace. First there was the Gentile centurion, whose armed presence represented the horror of pagan domination. Next was this childless widow, desolate and abandoned. Finally, there is the woman known for her scandalous sin, whose appearance ends this chapter. In chapter 6 Luke had presented Jesus' great sermon, in which he had taught, "Blessed are you who are poor, . . . blessed are you who hunger, . . . blessed are you who weep now" (vv. 21, 22), and this is a great theme all through this Gospel. All three of these outcast figures in Luke 7 illustrate that teaching, and they find grace from the Lord. The point is obvious—it is for the desolate, the lost, the despised that Jesus came as Savior. Jesus explained why this was so, saying, "It is not the healthy who need a doctor, but the sick. I have not come to call the righteous, but sinners" (Mark 2:17).

Of course, it is not just these figures of desolation who need God's grace but every one of us. This widow of Nain, trudging out with all her broken dreams and shattered plans, having lost not only her future but also her heart, well depicts this whole world. So far in our study of Jesus' miracles we have vividly seen the plight of humanity in this sinful, broken world: the leper in his disfiguring corruption, the paralytic unable to raise himself from his mat, and the centurion's servant beyond the help of any human physician. But now this scene, the hopeless widow taking out her son for burial, sums up them all, for death is the crown on which sickness and pain and alienation are merely dark jewels, the master to which they are mere servants. Because of death—both as it awaits us all in the end and as its principle of futility inhabits all our works—this world does not fulfill its promises, does not live up to its advertisements.

It doesn't matter what you pin your hopes to in this world, for they all lead to the same burial ground. To what have you attached your dreams? Is it romantic love? Love will betray you; if not sooner, then it will break your heart at death. Is it money or success? These too cannot go with you where death's door leads, nor can they satisfy the wants of the soul. Many people seem fixed upon their physical appearance and fitness. These are not bad things. And yet, "All men are like grass, and all their glory is like the flowers of the field" (Isa. 40:6). Ours is a mortal world, inflicted with God's curse on sin and rebellion, so that our only peace, our only rest, our only satisfaction, can be found in him.

Ours is a world dominated by the specter of death, and

DEATH = SIN

in such a funeral procession there will always be weeping, like this woman trudging again to the place of the dead. How well she depicts the problem of this world—death and sorrow and loss! It was for these that Jesus Christ came with words of comfort. Luke tells us, "When he saw her, his heart went out to her and he said, 'Don't cry.'" Or as I have put it, "Weep no more." This is what the gospel of Jesus Christ, the message of Christianity, is all about: a Savior who comes to the scene of death and of weeping with compassion, with comfort, and with power to save.

Life from the Dead

In our studies of the miracles, we have often had the occasion to observe the compassion of Jesus Christ, his sympathy for those who suffer, and his willingness to offer help. How often we give hollow, though well-meant, consolation to each other. But Luke shows us the uniqueness of our Lord through the comfort he alone was able to offer this poor widow. Luke tells us, "Then he went up and touched the coffin, and those carrying it stood still. He said, 'Young man, I say to you, get up!' The dead man sat up and began to talk, and Jesus gave him back to his mother" (7:14–15).

We remember that these miracles of Jesus are not isolated occasions of healing but are visual parables regarding his person and saving work. In that respect, few accounts tell us so much about Jesus as does this one.

First, Jesus went up and touched the pallet on which the dead man was lying. Luke, we remember, was a physician, and he was interested in details. This is the second time he has focused on Jesus touching something that was normally defiling. The first was when Jesus touched the leper, in all his horrid corruption. If there was anything

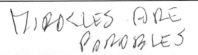
MIRACLES ARE PARABLES

worse in the Jewish ceremonial law than that, it was this—
touching a coffin or a person who was dead.

The whole point of the levitical restrictions, with their
focus on the clean and the unclean, was to distinguish between life and death, to separate them and to keep the
things of death far away from life, outside the camp and un-
touchable. That is why this procession was headed out
through the city gates, because death was taken outside the
camp, the same way the Old Testament describes the
damned being cast out in the final judgment, outside of and
away from the habitation of the redeemed (see Isa. 66:24).

With this matter of touching, Luke seems to be making
a point that connects to the whole ministry of Jesus Christ.
Martin Luther, in his sermon on this passage, thought so,
and he saw these two processions as typical of the two great
forces in this world. There was the procession of death and
darkness, with the widow at the head, followed by the body
and the mourners. Death, Luther reminds us, is the result of
sin and disobedience:

> When you hear the Scripture speaking of death, you
> must think not only of the grave and the coffin, and
> of the horrible manner in which life is separated
> from the body and how the body is destroyed and
> brought to naught, but you must think of the cause
> by which man is brought to death and without
> which death and that which accompanies it, would
> be impossible . . . namely, sin and the wrath of God
> on account of sin.[1]

No one dared to stop this procession; instead everyone
joined the crowd of mourners following behind the young
man's coffin. But coming in the other direction was Jesus

Christ—who Luke pointedly describes here as *the Lord*—and those who followed him; his is the procession of life and light. Jesus comes bearing a principle opposite to that of sin. He comes in righteousness. He comes bearing an opposing power to that of death—he comes with an unconquerable life. Therefore no case is hopeless to this Physician, not the centurion's servant who was near to death, and not even this young man who has actually died. Here is, Luther observes, "the true nature of Christ's work, showing why he came and reigns, namely, that he might destroy death and in its stead give life, as the prophet Isaiah, 25:8, says: 'He will swallow up death forever.'"[2]

The procession of death was moving steadily out of the city, out to the graveyard, when Jesus came up, saw the widow, and was moved to compassion. Approaching, he stopped the procession with the touch of his hand upon the open coffin. Luke is making a great point. Just as Jesus had touched the leper, just as he was willing to go into the Gentile centurion's home, Jesus is not defiled by the impure. He is not tainted by the touch of leprosy, by association with outcasts, by the chill of death. For he is the fountain of life; his purity and his cleanness overwhelm and wash away all sorts of filth, disease, alienation, and even death.

The significance of this does not fully unfold in Luke 7, but by the end of Luke's Gospel it does. Here we have a preview of Jesus' own death upon the cross. Then it was that he truly touched death, even embraced it for our sake. Jesus stepped forth now to comfort this widow in her desolation, and for this he came and took up our flesh, to remove all our sorrow by his death upon the cross. Paul writes in Galatians 3:13, "Christ redeemed us from the curse of the law by becoming a curse for us." Ours is a debt of sin that demands death, for "the wages of sin is death" (Rom. 6:23). Jesus gave himself to death to pay the price of our redemption. Again, it is Paul who writes, "God made him who had no sin to be sin for us, so that in him we might become the righteousness of God" (2 Cor. 5:21). *BE MADE*

Jesus took our disease, took our alienation, took our death upon himself at the cross. But it was not death that triumphed over Jesus; in his resurrection, death itself was conquered. As Paul wrote to Timothy, Jesus "destroyed death and has brought life and immortality to light" (2 Tim. 1:10) by his death and resurrection. That is what the New Testament proclaims with joy; that is what is prefigured in these scenes in the Gospels where Jesus raises the dead. Jesus is able to conquer death with life, and thus he overrules the death of this young man with his touch and his word.

The Word of Life

Jesus touched the coffin. He touched death and therefore is able to give true comfort to those who mourn. The second thing Luke tells us is that Jesus spoke to the dead man. What a remarkable statement that is: "Young man, I say to you, get up!" Because Jesus holds the power of life he can command even those who are dead. In John's Gospel he called out to his friend Lazarus, who lay in the tomb; here he speaks to this dead young man. In both cases, at the command of Jesus Christ, the dead came to life, one emerging from the tomb and the other from his coffin.

It had been a long time since the dead were raised in Israel. The crowd, as we see in Luke 7:16, identified Jesus as a great prophet, no doubt thinking back to Elijah and Elisha, the great prophets who had also given a dead son back to a widow. But there is a great difference between what they did and what Jesus here does. Elijah, when he healed the Shunammite widow's boy, did not himself raise the dead but cried out to God. First Kings 17:21 tells us, "Then he stretched himself out on the boy three times and cried to the LORD, 'O LORD my God, let this boy's life return to him!' " God answered that prayer, but there is a difference here when Jesus Christ raises the dead. Elijah spoke to God, praying for a miracle; Jesus acted as God and performed the resurrection wonder himself. He spoke to the dead man, and he brought him forth by his own power of life. Here is the Lord himself, to whose power Elijah had appealed. Here is God our Helper, bearing life into the world of death.

That is why God became flesh. That is why the Second Person of the eternal Trinity became man and entered this world, to comfort those who mourn. "Weep no more," Jesus said to the widow; but to say those words and offer more than mere sentiment, he came a very long way, from heaven to earth. He paid a very high price, even his death upon the cross. And it was in the same way, at the same cost, that he offers comfort to us. That is comfort indeed, the shed blood of the Son of God, beseeching us, "Weep no more."

Notice too how this saving work takes place in an individual life. Jesus speaks to the dead man, and with sovereign grace, with divine power, and without any human help, Jesus brings life to the dead. For everyone who has found comfort and salvation in Jesus Christ, it is only because he spoke to a dead man, to a dead woman. Paul writes, "You were dead in your transgressions and sins . . . by nature [an object] of wrath. But because of his great love for us, God, who is rich in mercy, made us alive with Christ even when we were dead in transgressions—it is by grace you have been saved" (Eph. 2:1–5).

Even now Jesus calls out through the gospel to all who

are dead in sin, dead in rebellion against the Lord of heaven, bound in chains of death and despair. And at his voice men and women come to life, they rejoice, they put their trust in him, they cease their weeping and turn to laughter, for their sins are forgiven and the life that is in Jesus becomes their own. The power of life is in the voice of our Savior, calling those dead in sin to life in him. That is the mark of Christ's divine power at work in this world. Geerhardus Vos observes:

> It is a call like the voice of God at the first creation, "Let there be light," and there was light. . . . This is that wonderful effectual calling by name, which takes place wherever a sinner is saved. . . . For it is characteristic of God, and of God alone, thus to produce effects by mere word. He gives life to the dead and calls the things that are not, as though they were.[3]

Life in an Age of Death

But Jesus' work is not yet done. There are still tears; there is much cause for weeping. We will yet cry over sickness and fear and death. All that this miracle shows us, all that we see and experience in the church as dead souls are brought to spiritual life, is still a foretaste of that great work that is yet to be finished. The apostle Paul reminds us who live in this age of expectation: "For he must reign until he has put all his enemies under his feet. The last enemy to be destroyed is death" (1 Cor. 15:25–26).

Christ's work in history is not yet finished, and so death, though defeated, is not yet banished. But for the believer, for now, Christ has removed its sting by the power of his resurrection. "The sting of death is sin, and the power of sin is the law" (1 Cor. 15:56). Yes, there is death but not its power to condemn or destroy. Thomas Watson explains how the resurrection transforms our view of death, after which comes glory for all who are in Christ: "Death smites a believer as the angel did Peter, and made his chains fall off (Acts 12:7). . . . Oh! what a blessed privilege is this, to be without spot or wrinkle; to be purer than the sunbeams; to be as free from sin as the angels! (Eph. 5:27)."[4]

Even the small and daily deaths we experience are but God's refinement of dross into gold, the process of life by which we must decrease and Christ must increase. And yet that day will come when Christ's enemies all are put away. Revelation 20:14 tells us of its coming: "Then death and Hades were thrown into the lake of fire." Then will reign the new creation, in which there will be neither death nor tears. In the new heavens and new earth, born of Christ's resurrection, these words from the last chapter of the Bible will have come true: "And I heard a loud voice from the throne saying, 'Now the dwelling of God is with men, and he will live with them. They will be his people, and God himself will be with them and be their God. He will wipe every tear from their eyes. There will be no more death or mourning or crying or pain, for the old order of things has passed away'" (Rev. 21:3–4).

"Weep no more," says Jesus to those who mourn. In those words is great comfort, for they are accompanied by a great and saving action. For now we are comforted, but when life has finally and fully triumphed over death, we not only will cease our weeping but also will receive back beauty for all our ashes. That is the last thing we see in this lovely picture. "Jesus gave him back to his mother" (Luke 7:15). So shall it be for all who seek comfort in him. All our sorrow will be returned as gladness, all our loss with heavenly fullness, all our weeping with songs of praise. As Charles Haddon Spurgeon commented on this wonderful scene outside the gates of Nain:

> This was a rehearsal upon a small scale of that which shall happen by-and-by, when those who are in their graves shall hear the voice of the Son of God and live: then shall the last enemy be destroyed. Only let death come into contact with him who is our life, and it is compelled to relax its hold, whatever may be the spoil which it has captured. Soon shall our Lord come in his glory, and then before the gates of the New Jerusalem we shall see the miracle at the gates of Nain multiplied a myriad times.[5]

Praise to the Lord

The account concludes with the marvel of all those who stood watching. "They were all filled with awe and praised God. 'A great prophet has appeared among us,' they said. 'God has come to help his people'" (Luke 7:16). And they spread the news all through the country.

That is exactly how we too should respond. A great prophet—the One to whom all the prophets pointed—has come to bring help from God to earth. Undoubtedly the people thought back to Elijah and Elisha, both of whom had raised a widow's son in the Old Testament. The thought of such a prophet in their midst filled them with wonder and with praise for God. That is exactly how we should feel. We should be awestruck at such a Savior and filled with praise to God for what he has provided to us in the gospel.

"Weep no more," he says. Jesus looks with this great compassion upon all of us who are downcast in spirit, who are brokenhearted, who are lost in suffering and sorrow. He does not belittle our tears; far from it. He does not deny the cause of our anguish, for he himself knows it full well. He has tasted the bitter dregs of life in this world. So when he says to us, "Do not cry," it is because he has reached out with his own hand to touch the source of our tears, to take it to his cross, so that he might speak to us with words of life. Every one of us should know in our trials and sorrows that God looks upon us with eyes that are wet with compassion. Jesus knows what it is to sorrow; his own eyes were often reddened with tears. As Scripture teaches, "Because he himself suffered when he was tempted, he is able to help those who are being tempted" (Heb. 2:18).

God has provided the very thing we need but could not gain for ourselves. That is what this miracle shows us. Jesus Christ breaks into the funeral procession that awaits us all, and he calls out this great promise: "I am the resurrection and the life. He who believes in me will live, even though he dies; and whoever lives and believes in me will never die" (John 11:25–26).

So do you weep? Think back to that biblical parade of tears, the various causes for weeping that one way or another you share. Yes, you do weep, and you will. But Jesus comes and says, "Weep no more," and so not one of our tears should ever fall to the ground without hope, even without joy of what lies ahead, and without an eye lifted up to Jesus and to that great day coming when all our tears will be no more.

6

Lord of the Storm

Luke 8:22–25

The disciples went and woke him, saying, "Master, Master, we're going to drown!" He got up and rebuked the wind and the raging waters; the storm subsided, and all was calm. "Where is your faith?" he asked his disciples. (Luke 8:24–25)

One of my favorite series of Bible storybooks for children is by Ella K. Lindvall, who presents a number of biblical stories in detail and with vivid illustrations. One particular drawing in her books captivated me when I first saw it, and it still does. I confess that I often choose this book to read to my children and linger at this scene. There is a boat seen in the distance with what looks like a number of men huddled together and one man dressed in white standing erect. His arms are outstretched, and, though he is far enough away that it is hard to tell, he seems utterly composed. All around him, filling the picture frame, are flat, calm seas, reflecting the peaceful sky above. As far as the eye can see in all directions is peace, calm, a pregnant stillness. It is not a scene from nature, which knows no calm like this. Rather, it is a startling portrayal of the divine peace that is the particular mark of the presence of Jesus Christ.

The words that go with this picture are his words: "Peace, be still." That is what he commanded to the swirling winds and the frantic waves. At his voice even they obeyed, and stillness was all around. He is Lord over the storm, the bringer of heavenly peace to the raging seas of earth. Jesus commanded the elements and, as Luke tells us in this account, "all was calm." As one commentator observes, it was "a mysterious, supernatural calm that testified to the sovereign power of Jesus but also the deep peace and security that belong to those who follow Him."[1]

Upon Stormy Seas

That is what this miracle account is about, both the sovereign, divine power of the Lord Jesus Christ and the peace he brings to all who trust in him. There are four main teaching points in this passage, the first of which is this: those who follow and serve Jesus Christ must pass through storms in this life.

That is a lesson learned by the original disciples. They were with the Lord, they had been serving him all this time, they had left everything to follow him. This is not a picture of men "out of the center of God's will," as people sometimes put it today. They were with the Lord, and yet they passed through a terrible storm, a great danger that brought terror into their hearts and threatened their lives. This is what we can expect also, not in spite of, but because we travel in company with Jesus Christ through this world. Charles Haddon Spurgeon compares this boat with the church:

> We see in the church a vessel bearing rich cargo, steering for a desired haven, and fitted out for fishing on the road, should fair opportunity occur . . . I scarcely know of an apter picture of a church than a ship upon the treacherous Galilean Sea with Jesus and His disciples sailing in it. . . . Every sail of the good ship which bears the flag of the High Admiral of our fleet must be beaten with the wind, and every plank in her must be tried by the waves.[2]

From the early days of New Testament interpretation the boat in this story was taken as a type of the church, with two great sources of trial, much like these winds and waves. The first of these is heresy, which often has come close to wrecking the ship of the church. Second, there is persecution. Like the spray that flew in the faces of these disciples, the tears and the blood of the martyrs have flown about in the winds of this terrible storm. It has always been so, and it is so today; in one place or another at least one of these two afflictions is sure to be found so that the church has never sailed free from peril.

What is true for the church as a whole is also true for individual Christians. The Scriptures teach us that in this world we will suffer all kinds of trials. This is what Paul and Barnabas taught in their missionary travels. Acts 14:22 quotes them saying, "We must go through many hardships to enter the kingdom of God." The apostle Peter put it bluntly in his first epistle: "Dear friends, do not be surprised at the painful trial you are suffering, as though something

strange were happening to you. But rejoice that you participate in the sufferings of Christ, so that you may be over-
joyed when his glory is revealed" (1 Peter 4:12–13).

There are two reasons why this is so, both of which can
be seen in this account. The first reason is *the environment
in which our pilgrimage takes place*. This is an important thing
for us to realize, lest we be caught unawares in the world.
Today's advertisers would have us believe that we live in an
amusement park, a place where all is safe and everything
can be tried and tasted without danger or harm. Most people think of life as a great shopping mall, a place where we
are supposed to be in control and everything caters to our
whims. And yet our experience tells us that neither of these
is a true description of where we live.

The Bible is quite sober in its description of this world.
The Book of Genesis tells us, for instance, that we no longer
live in the garden with its fertile delights, but east of Eden,
in the sin-blasted world where thorns grow and hostile forces
prowl. One of the main New Testament descriptions of this
life is that of the wilderness. Christians have been delivered
from the bondage of Egypt—that is good—but have not yet
arrived safely in the land of promise. The wilderness is a
place of danger and of testing, an environment where we perish unless we make use of the resources God provides.

This passage gives us another description of where we
live—the storm-swept sea. The Sea of Galilee is located in
a great depression some seven hundred feet below sea level
and ringed by hills, many of which are quite steep. When
the cold air descends from Mount Hermon's crown at
ninety-two hundred feet above sea level and crashes down
against the warm air at the level of the lake, massive winds
and sudden storms are often the result. These can occur
suddenly and with brutal force.

The whole world in which we live is much like that. It is a tempestuous environment that is especially hostile to the passage of Christians. Many a storm arises across our path, whether subtle scorn or outright persecution, whether the allure of things that glitter or the flaring lusts of the flesh or the urge to self-indulgence and sloth. Christians have often isolated three main threats that afflict us in this life, the world, the flesh, and the devil, all of which ever conspire to catch us unawares.

It is worth noting that the Old Testament commonly used the seething torrent of the sea as a symbol of the forces hostile to God and his people. In Psalm 69, for instance, David cries out:

> Save me, O God,
>> for the waters have come up to my neck . . .
> deliver me from those who hate me,
>> from the deep waters.
> Do not let the floodwaters engulf me
>> or the depths swallow me up. (vv. 1, 14–15)

This is how Christians will feel from time to time in this world, as forces hostile to faith and godliness assail us suddenly and fiercely. We cannot avoid trouble and trial, simply because of the environment in which we live.

There is a second reason, however, that we will experience trials, and it too is seen here. This reason is that *Jesus himself sends us out into the storms.* This passage begins with him saying, "Let's go over to the other side of the lake" (Luke 8:22), knowing full well what lay ahead. His purpose is to test our faith. That is why God sent Israel into the desert en route to Canaan, and this is why Jesus sends us out into stormy seas. In our earlier study of the centurion who believed, we noted that faith is what Jesus is looking for in this world; faith is what he marvels at. When the storm had been conquered, the character of the disciples' faith drew his comment: "Where is your faith?" he asked them (Luke 8:25). This is what Peter, who after all was in this boat, later passed on in his first epistle. Speaking of trials, he wrote, "These have come so that your faith—of greater worth than gold, which perishes even though refined by fire—may be proved genuine and may result in praise, glory and honor when Jesus Christ is revealed" (1 Peter 1:7).

For these reasons, all Christians will pass through sudden and fierce storms, not in spite of our fellowship with Jesus but because of it. We enter tribulations because it is the nature of our hostile environment and because our Lord wants to test and strengthen our faith in him. J. C. Ryle observes:

> By affliction He teaches us many precious lessons, which, without it we should never learn. By affliction He shows us our emptiness and weakness, draws us to the throne of grace, purifies our affections, weans us from the world, and makes us long for heaven. In the resurrection morning we shall all say, 'it is good for me that I was afflicted.' We shall thank God for every storm.[3]

Christ's Commanding Power

The second lesson this passage strikingly teaches is the commanding power of the Lord Jesus Christ. Our first clue to this is that he lay sleeping during the tumult of this storm. There was a reason for this calmness: this storm was no threat to him. But it was after the disciples woke him that his power to save was truly revealed: "The boat was being swamped, and they were in great danger. The disciples went and woke him, saying, 'Master, Master, we're going to drown!' He got up and rebuked the wind and the raging waters; the storm subsided, and all was calm" (Luke 8:23–24).

Once again it is the voice of Jesus Christ that delivers his power. In the last chapter Jesus spoke to a dead man, who then arose alive. Now he speaks to the winds and the waves. Indeed, Luke emphasizes that Jesus "rebuked" the wind and the raging waters." Some commentators have suggested that this indicates a demonic presence within these elements, but that is not a necessary inference. Rather, they are personified in a figurative sense, inasmuch as the Lord has authority over them. What this shows is the power of Christ over the hostile forces we rightly fear. Even the elements know the voice of their Master, and when he commands they cannot but obey.

It is hard to imagine a more striking display of sovereign power than this. When it comes to the raising of the dead, we are dealing in a realm where we are used to seeing human deliverances. Doctors return patients at least from the brink of death, if not from the grave as Jesus does. There the difference is largely one of degree. But here we have a difference in kind. No one can command the winds and the waves, and yet Jesus does. He is therefore in a class by himself. Mark's Gospel tells us his words: "Peace, be still!" And at his command the winds died down and all was quiet upon the waters.

Surely this example tells us that there is no circumstance we might face over which Jesus Christ lacks authority and power. Is it physical danger like this? Then Jesus demonstrates his complete ability to deliver us from any peril. Is it devastating news of an unexpected sickness or some other circumstance we lack the strength to endure,

some temptation we lack strength to oppose? What an encouragement this is to draw near in prayer in times of trouble. Christ commands the elements with the voice of his
power; when we look to him, calm arises on the face of our
circumstances.

Seeing what happened on this lake, we remember what
the angels had foretold at the time of his birth: "Glory to
God in the highest, and on earth peace to men on whom
his favor rests" (Luke 2:14). Jesus came to bring peace.
First, he brings peace between God and humanity. That is
what Paul emphasized in Romans 5:1—"Since we have
been justified through faith, we have peace with God
through our Lord Jesus Christ." This was why Jesus came
into the world, to bear our sins on the cross and reconcile
us to God. But having done that, Christ offers peace in our
hearts, even in the storms of this life. This is why we are to
be eager to call out to him in prayer, seeking a peace that
comes only by hearing his voice. Paul wrote about this, saying, "Do not be anxious about anything, but in everything,
by prayer and petition, with thanksgiving, present your requests to God. And the peace of God, which transcends all
understanding, will guard your hearts and your minds in
Christ Jesus" (Phil. 4:6–7).

It is the special work of the Holy Spirit to give us this
peace as we trust in Christ. He says, "Peace I leave with
you; my peace I give you. I do not give to you as the world
gives. Do not let your hearts be troubled, and do not be
afraid" (John 14:27).

Who Is This Man?

This brings us to the third lesson from this passage,
which is best approached with a question. It is a question

Luke is moving toward in his Gospel, a question later asked of the disciples by Jesus himself. When this question finally comes, it serves as a turning point in the whole Gospel of Luke. We find it in chapter 9, where Jesus says to the disciples, "Who do the crowds say I am?" That was a fairly safe question, having to do with other people's opinions, and the disciples were ready with the various answers. "Some say John the Baptist; others say Elijah; and still others, that one of the prophets of long ago has come back to life." But then Jesus made the question quite a bit more personal, turning directly to them and saying, "But what about you? . . . Who do you say I am?" (Luke 9:18–20).

That is the question each of us must answer. What about you? Who do you say he is? Jesus' question and Peter's subsequent answer in chapter 9 is a turning point in Luke's Gospel. It is also a turning point in the lives of all to whom that question comes. That crucial turning point is anticipated in this passage, when the disciples asked it of one another. "Who is this?" they cried. "He commands even the winds and the water, and they obey him" (Luke 8:25).

This miracle account offers two important answers to that great question. The first answer is that Jesus Christ is a man, fully capable of experiencing all our weakness and infirmity and depending upon God's protection and care with an absolute faith.

That is what we find as the passage begins. Jesus directs the disciples into the boat and heads them for the far shore. Immediately as they sailed, he fell asleep. His was a body like our own that hungered and thirsted, that felt pain and fatigue, that required sleep to go on. Surely he needed rest, for Jesus had been wearying himself much in the labor his Father had given to him.

In that respect, Jesus is the greatest example of the life

of faith. Look at the calm with which he confided himself to God. There is the sign of one who knows the Lord: that he rests securely in the fiercest storm. Our own knowledge of and personal acquaintance with God will have that effect in our lives. But surely there was never anyone who better exemplified the words of Psalm 91 than Jesus:

> He who dwells in the shelter of the Most High
>   will rest in the shadow of the Almighty.
> I will say of the LORD, "He is my refuge and my
>   fortress,
>   my God, in whom I trust." (vv. 1–2)

The peace he would soon impose upon the storm is one that came from within his own heart; it is out of his own peace that he brings peace to the world.

What was true in the boat was brought to its climax when Jesus was hanging upon the cross. There, as he willingly laid down his life for us, Jesus cried out, "Father, into your hands I commit my spirit" (Luke 23:46). So ought we, following after him, commit ourselves to Almighty God for the much lesser crosses we must bear as we pass through this life.

Jesus in his full humanity is the ultimate *example for our faith*, but here we also see him in all his divinity, as the *object of our faith*. If anything, this is the great emphasis in this passage, in which we see Jesus Christ fully and stunningly identified with the Lord of the Old Testament, even with the divine name Jehovah or Yahweh. Perhaps more clearly here than any place else, we see all that in the Old Testament was attributed to Yahweh alone now applied to the person of our Lord Jesus Christ. This is the second answer to the question Who is Jesus Christ? He is the Lord.

The raging sea symbolizes the creation in revolt against God. The stormy waters embrace all the rebellion of this world against the Creator, the God of order and peace. And here we see Jesus, the God-Man, standing erect in the storm and calling out with the voice of power, "Peace, be still!" We can only think back to great passages in the Old Testament, like that of Psalm 29, which says,

> The voice of the LORD is over the waters;
>   the God of glory thunders,
>   the LORD thunders over the mighty waters.
> The voice of the LORD is powerful;
>   the voice of the LORD is majestic. (vv. 3–4)

That is the Old Testament's awesome picture of Yahweh in all his might, and here it is directly manifested in the life of Jesus Christ.

Psalm 89 says,

> O LORD God Almighty, who is like you?
>   You are mighty, O LORD, and your faithfulness
>   surrounds you.
> You rule over the surging sea;
>   when its waves mount up, you still them. (vv. 8–9)

Similarly, Psalm 107 tells us:

> Then they cried out to the LORD in their trouble,
>   and he brought them out of their distress.
> He stilled the storm to a whisper;
>   the waves of the sea were hushed.
> They were glad when it grew calm,
>   and he guided them to their desired haven.

> Let them give thanks to the LORD for his unfailing
> love
> and his wonderful deeds for men. (vv. 28–31)

In light of these passages, everything that can be said about the Lord God of the Old Testament, Yahweh is his name, can be equally applied to the person of this Jesus Christ. Who is he? The answer is clear. He is the Lord; he is God in our midst, the Lord Almighty.

That is what the Old Testament says about Jesus Christ, but let's make the question personal. Who do you say he is? Do not say that the Bible presents Jesus Christ as just another wise man, one who never made great claims about himself, never took on the mantle of God. That option is not available in light of this passage. This scene on the lake is either false, a monstrous hoax, or it compels us to acknowledge him, to worship him as Lord and God. But it is not a hoax. It is attested to by eyewitnesses, even participants like Matthew, who speaks of this in his own Gospel. It was published as an account of a highly public event; Mark tells us there were other boats that went out with them (4:36). As Paul said about Jesus' death, so also here: this thing "was not done in a corner" (Acts 26:26). The claims of this miracle account could not be sustained if it were a mere invention. It is a true account, written while many were still living who could refute any frauds but who also could validate what Luke tells us. As such, it obliges us to proclaim that Jesus is not just another religious cult figure, not just an admirable moralist. He is the Lord, who alone can bring peace to the earth, who commands the elements and commands our allegiance as well.

"Who do you say that I am?" That was the question Jesus pressed upon the disciples, who had been through this experience with him and many others. In Luke 9 we read of what is called the great confession from the lips of Simon Peter. He was the first one to give the right answer: "You are the Christ of God." Included in that statement is this: "You are the Messiah, the Anointed One promised to come and save and deliver."

That is the true confession regarding Jesus Christ, and unless it is your confession, his work is of no benefit to you. "Believe on the Lord Jesus Christ, and you will be saved," says the Scripture. But if you do not believe on him, if you do not proclaim him Lord and Savior of your own life, if you do not cry out to him for salvation, then you will be drowned in the torrent of your sins and overcome by the raging wind of God's wrath in the day of his judgment.

Peace That Passes Understanding

That leads to a fourth and final observation, that faith in Christ is the only means of real peace in this world.

That is why this passage focuses on the faith of the disciples. It was faith that Jesus was interested in. He did not comment on the terror of the storm, for it was no surprise to him. He did not boast regarding his wondrous work. What drew his notice was what the storm revealed about their faith. Why is that? Because it is by faith that we are saved, by faith that we are made strong, and by faith that we receive the peace he came to give. We think it is astonishing miracles that glorify Jesus most, but he thinks our faith gives him the most glory and pleasure. It is our faith that Jesus marvels at with joy.

If this was a test of faith it was not one that produced high marks for the disciples. "Where is your faith?" Jesus complained. Giving us a more complete account, Mark

puts it this way: "Why are you so afraid? Do you still have
no faith?" (4:40).

On the surface of things it is hard to see why Jesus
would say this. The storm was too great for the disciples to
bear on their own, and the danger was real. Luke tells us,
"The boat was being swamped, and they were in great danger" (8:23). The problem was not that they turned to Jesus
or called out to him. Indeed, it is noteworthy that while the
crashing waves and howling wind did not rouse our Lord,
the cries of his sheep did awaken the Good Shepherd. It
was no surprise and no failure of faith for them to have summoned him.

The problem was the attitude with which they summoned him, the panicked and hysterical fear that revealed
not just their need of him but also their lack of trust. Luke
tells us that they cried, "Master, Master, we're going to
drown!" Mark's Gospel again supplies other helpful details.
Some of them awoke Jesus with an accusation: "Teacher,
don't you care if we drown?" (Mark 4:38).

It is not to our shame if we are frightened in danger or
that we hasten to call upon him who cares for the flock. But
the faith that trusts him implicitly picks up the words of
Psalm 23 and with quiet repose expresses its comfort:

> Even though I walk
>   through the valley of the shadow of death,
> I will fear no evil,
>   for you are with me;
> your rod and your staff,
>   they comfort me. (v. 4)

That is the faith that Jesus was looking for, the faith we
need in the storms of our own lives, storms that often spring

up unannounced and uninvited and yet are our lot in this world. Through faith in Jesus Christ, the Lord of the storm, ours is the peace that passes understanding, as he guards our hearts and minds with his Word and Spirit.

I know of no better example of this than the experience of a believer named Horatio Spafford, in the storm that beset him in 1873. He was a successful lawyer in Chicago, a devoted Christian, and a strong supporter of the evangelistic ministry of Dwight L. Moody. In 1871 his only son had died, and then in the Great Fire he lost a good deal of his fortune in real estate. Anxious to get away from these troubles and eager to help Moody in a revival he had scheduled in England, Spafford purchased tickets for himself, his wife, and his four daughters on a ship sailing across the Atlantic.

Just before the voyage was to begin, Spafford was delayed by urgent business, so he sent off his family, intending to follow after a few days. However, in the voyage their ship was struck by another vessel and sank beneath the waves in only a few short minutes. Several days went by with no news, until finally a cable arrived from his wife. It read, "Saved alone."

Brokenhearted, Spafford followed on the next available ship, no doubt peering out into the waves for many a long night. Passing through a certain stretch of sea, he apparently was informed that this was very nearly the spot where his four beloved daughters had gone down into the deep. Imagine what storms must have raged within his soul, and yet with eyes fixed upon the Lord he discovered a great peace, resting upon the finished work of Jesus Christ. Taking out pen and paper, Spafford then wrote down the words to this great hymn:

When peace, like a river, attendeth my way.
When sorrows like sea billows roll.

Whatever my lot, Thou has taught me to say:
"It is well, it is well with my soul."

Though Satan should buffet, though trials should
      come,
Let this blest assurance control.
That Christ hath regarded my helpless estate,
And hath shed His own blood for my soul.

That is the peace that comes when Jesus asks us, "Who do you say that I am?" and we respond in faith, "You are the Christ, you are the Savior of my soul. You are the Redeemer who has purchased me from my sins and destined me for a peace that transcends every trial in this storm-blasted world." That is the great confession demanded by this passage, and it stilled the waves in Horatio Spafford's tortured soul.

Spafford began his hymn looking back to Christ, who died on the cross for him, but he finished by looking forward beyond the storms, beyond the horizon, to another land, another shore on which his children had already landed in safety. We too will often gaze to that distant beach that draws nearer every day, like that to which Jesus and the disciples were headed in the boat, the destination toward which the church of Christ sails even now beneath his streaming banner. And thus Spafford concluded the hymn with these lovely words born of the peace that comes from Christ alone:

O Lord, haste the day when my faith shall be
      sight,
The clouds be rolled back as a scroll,
The trump shall resound and the Lord shall descend;
Even so—it is well with my soul.

I do not think it is trite to observe that he saw Jesus Christ in the boat with him, and that is why it was well with his soul. He saw the Lord who stands before the storm, whose voice can calm the winds and tame the waves.

Do you see Jesus Christ and his saving presence in your trials? If you do not, there will be no voice to calm the storm. That is where the answer to your trouble is found, where safety will be discovered. Let us then reflect upon Jesus, submit our troubled hearts to him in prayer, in meditation, in conversation. If you ask, he will give to you the faith that he is looking for, that pleases and honors him, and that will save your soul. "Who can this be?" you then will marvel, as he leads you safely through the storms of this life. "Even the winds and the waves obey him!"

"Peace, be still!" commands Jesus Christ. It is not just the waves he commands; he speaks to us, no less than the storm. Be still, hear his voice, trust in him who is the Lord of every circumstance, every storm, every trial, every affliction, working for our good and for his glory. And when you receive that peace through faith, when you display that supernatural calm before the watching eyes of this world, a peace it can neither understand nor deny, you no less than the waves on that Galilean sea will bear testimony to who he is, to the sovereign majesty, the saving grace of him who is the Lord of the storm, so that others too will believe.

Humanity Restored

Luke 8:26–39

*When he saw Jesus, he cried out and fell at his feet, shouting
at the top of his voice, "What do you want with me, Jesus,
Son of the Most High God? I beg you, don't torture me!"
For Jesus had commanded the evil spirit to come
out of the man. Many times it had seized him, and though
he was chained hand and foot and kept under guard,
he had broken his chains and had been driven by the
demon into solitary places.* (Luke 8:28–29)

In his best-selling book *People of the Lie*, psychiatrist M. Scott
Peck describes his growing acceptance of the reality of evil,
and even of the devil and demonic possession. He describes
his four-year-long attempt to treat a woman named Charlene. Despite all his best efforts, Charlene was completely
resistant to help or care. Peck ultimately came to the con-

clusion that this woman was evil, a diagnosis she did not quarrel with. In retrospect, he concludes that all along her supposed quest for therapy was nothing more than an attempt to devour him. He writes, "Charlene's desire to make a conquest of me, to toy with me, to utterly control our relationship, knew no bounds. It seemed to be a desire for power purely for its own sake. . . . Her thirst for power was unsubordinated to anything higher than itself."[1]

One telling moment occurred when Peck asked her what she thought the meaning of life was. Recalling that she had been raised in the Christian church and had served as a Sunday school teacher, he thought she must have received some answer there. Charlene candidly replied that she had been taught that the meaning of life is to glorify God. But then she vehemently went on to add, "I cannot do it. There's no room for me in that. That would be my death. I don't want to live for God. I will not. I want to live for me. My own sake!"[2]

His experience with Charlene and with others caused Peck to rethink the idea of the demonic, which he had previously rejected with typically modern skepticism. Now open to the possibility, Peck sought out cases of demon possession, and in his book he states that he found two genuine cases of satanic possession, both of which were overcome by the power of God.

This does not come as a surprise to those who believe the teaching of the Bible, in this case as especially found in the Gospel accounts of the ministry of Jesus Christ. The Gospels are filled with confrontations between Jesus and the demons, and these battles give us perhaps the most pointed understanding of his ministry. "If I drive out demons by the finger of God," Jesus said, "then the kingdom of God has come to you" (Luke 11:20). The account in Luke 8:26–39, which we will consider in this chapter, presents one of the most developed and dramatic of these confrontations. It shows us that Jesus' miracles were an in-breaking of the kingdom of God at the expense of the kingdom of Satan, while also exposing the destructive design of sin and of the devil. Finally, it wonderfully portrays Christian salvation as the restoration of humanity as God lovingly designed and intended.

Questions about Demons

When we are talking about the subject of demon possession there are always two errors we can make, the first of which is to write off or deny the existence of supernatural beings like the devil and demons, as well as their impact in our world. The Bible flatly asserts the existence of Satan and the demons who serve him; there is no question in the Gospel accounts that Jesus acknowledged them, and if you are going to accept the Bible at face value then you will have to accept the reality of these spiritual powers. The denial of the supernatural as a whole, and therefore of Satan and the demons, is especially associated with modernity and its naturalism. It was this naturalistic skepticism that Peck was forced to reexamine in light of his experience. But he is not the only one forced to consider the reality of personified evil. I believe that the evidence of just the twentieth century points to an organized evil in this world that even determined modernists will find hard to account for except in personified spiritual evil.

What about the question, Are people possessed by demons in our own time? Apart from showing that demon possession is a real phenomenon and giving us descriptions, the Bible doesn't answer this. There is no reason, however, for us to doubt that it remains a real phenomenon, and credible accounts are not hard to find, like those from Peck. I, like many other Christians, have heard credible, first-hand reports from missionaries in places where the occult is a serious and open force. In America there is perhaps less need for outright possession, since Satan's cause of evil is so well served by the widely accepted value systems of materialism and sensuality, by hatred and greed and lust. However, I think there is reason to believe that the increased openness to the occult in America will likely usher in an increasingly overt satanism. You cannot help but notice the increased presence of psychic shops and the availability of occult services. To toy with these is to open yourself to demonic powers. Both of the possessions Peck describes began with a dabbling in the occult.

Another question that people bring up is this: Why was there so much demon possession in Jesus' time compared with all the other eras of the Bible? It is true that you find virtually none of what Jesus dealt with in the Old Testament. Saul was afflicted by an evil spirit (1 Sam. 16:14), but mostly the demonic appears as the powers lurking behind the idolatrous religions opposed to Israel. When Moses confronted Pharaoh with God's power, the Egyptians had their own wonderworkers (Ex. 7:11–12). They were charlatans and counterfeits, and they were easily overcome by God's might, but it was real power they employed and impressive to mortals.

Why so much demon possession in the time of Jesus? I think it is the same principle by which a magnet draws out its polar opposite. As we shall see, the demons understood very much about Jesus, and in response to his coming Satan concentrated his forces to oppose him. That makes sense to me, but there is also an explanation offered by Charles

Haddon Spurgeon that I think strikes close to the mark. Spurgeon points out that Satan never has anything of his own to offer; his is always a counterfeit of what God has done and is doing. Having observed the marvelous miracle of the incarnation, in which God came to dwell on earth veiled in flesh in Jesus Christ, Satan would have been motivated to attempt the same.[3] That perhaps is why we find so much demon possession during Jesus' first advent.

All of that comes under the heading of believing and explaining the presence of demon possession in the Gospel accounts, in response to the error of unbelief. There is another error, however, that I think is prevalent today. This is the error not of denying the supernatural and demons but of becoming overly fixated on them. This is the attitude displayed in many popular novels. What one must do as a Christian, this view insinuates, is be aware of the clashing swords of angels versus demons, to throw your resources into the fight and collaborate with the invisible forces of light against the darkness that surrounds you.

But the New Testament nowhere urges us to speculate on the happenings of the spiritual realm. Yes, passages like Ephesians 6 acknowledge "spiritual forces of evil in the heavenly realms" (v. 12). But when Paul says that "our struggle is not against flesh and blood, but against the rulers, against the authorities, against the powers of this dark world," that does not mean that we are to pit ourselves against demons directly. Rather, we are to reject sin, to oppose the value systems of Satan's pernicious influence—lust and greed, anger and hate. We wage spiritual warfare not by fighting demons but by dealing with the sin in us, by fleeing temptation, and by becoming more godly through the exercise of faith in Christ.

Therefore the Scriptures tell us not to focus on personified spiritual forces but on the redemptive work of Jesus Christ. The question is not whether we can deal with demonic powers—this account in Luke before us makes clear that we cannot—but whether God can. Is he able to handle the deepest depths of darkness as they are afoot in this world? Is Christ's saving work sufficient both to redeem and restore those bound and scarred and twisted by evil? That is where our focus should be—on Christ and his redeeming work—and that is where this passage focuses us as well.

This story offers three vital portraits dealing with the victory of Christ and his kingdom, which we will consider in order: a portrait of Satan's reign, or the reign of sin, and its effects on humankind; a portrait of Christ's saving work both in its power and its redeeming purpose; and a portrait of Jesus Christ as the missionary Savior come to restore lost humankind.

A Portrait of Satan's Reign of Sin

Our passage begins with a description of this man possessed by demons (Luke 8:27–29). He is barely recognizable as a human being, more closely resembling a beast than a man. Jesus and his disciples encountered this man after they had crossed the lake into the Gentile regions on the eastern shore. It seems that the location was near the village of Gerasa in the district known by the local capital of Gadara; ancient tombs dug into the hillside can still be seen there.

> When Jesus stepped ashore, he was met by a demon-possessed man from the town. For a long time this man had not worn clothes or lived in a house, but had lived in the tombs. . . . Many times it [the evil

spirit] had seized him, and though he was chained hand and foot and kept under guard, he had broken his chains and had been driven by the demon into solitary places. (Luke 8:27–29)

Luke tells us four things about this demon-possessed man. First, he was naked. Second, he lived in solitary places, having been driven there by the demon, even though the man was chained and guarded. Third, Luke tells us of a supernatural and bestial strength, by which he freed himself from these bonds. Fourth, we are told that he frequented the places of the dead, living not just in the wilds but among tombs. This story is recounted in two other Gospels, where we learn additional details. Matthew tells us that he, along with at least one other demoniac, made this area impassable to travelers (8:28). Mark adds, "Night and day among the tombs and in the hills he would cry out and cut himself with stones" (5:5).

It is hard to imagine a more pathetic and revolting portrayal of what had once been a man. He now was twisted and degraded and destroyed; perhaps his penchant for tombs reflects either the living death he experienced or his frantic desire for death as a means of escape. As it is, he was restless in his anguish, miserable in his exposure, violent in his every act.

What we are seeing is a vivid portrayal of what Satan's rule means for humankind, a foretaste of hell itself. Here is a replay of what happened to Adam and Eve in the fall, with the effects only amplified by this demon possession. Led by the serpent, Adam and Eve sinned and rebelled against God and therefore fell from blessing to the cursed state we see so advanced and concentrated in this demoniac. Created in God's own image, he now reflects the character of demons; called to fruitful employment, he stalks and destroys; intended for outward righteousness and inward bliss, the demoniac is naked and horrid, restless and anguished of body and soul. Commissioned to multiply in abundance and life, he lives in solitude, lingering as close to death as he is able.

What brought this man so low were the demons that possessed him. Similarly, it is by the work of Satan that the human race has been distorted and degraded through bondage to sin. What we see here in this portrait is but a concentrated manifestation of the entire reign of Satan and sin. The human story that began with the charge, "Be fruitful, and multiply" (Gen. 1:28 KJV), has devolved into a situation best described by the words of God's curse to Cain, the first murderer, "You will be a restless wanderer on the earth" (Gen. 4:12). So it is even today.

Let me anticipate an objection that many people will offer to this assessment. They reply that they are not followers of the devil. They do not participate in bizarre rituals. They may even belong to a church. They are just trying to get along in the world, so this picture has nothing to do with them. But this way of thinking is dangerously wrong. The apostle Paul answers this objection in the letter to the Ephesians, where he insists that apart from Christ we are all under Satan's dominion and reign. Writing to Christians, he says:

> As for you, you were dead in your transgressions and sins, in which you used to live when you followed the ways of this world and of the ruler of the kingdom of the air, the spirit who is now at work in those who are disobedient. All of us also lived among them at one time, gratifying the cravings of

our sinful nature and following its desires and thoughts. (Eph. 2:1–3)

That is what it means to live in thrall to the devil. You do not have to be demon possessed like this man; you do not have to visit a psychic shop or participate in bizarre ceremonies. You do not have to even believe in or acknowledge Satan in any way—indeed, so much the better for him if you do not. If you follow the ways of this world, if you gratify the sinful nature with its cravings and desires and thoughts, you are doing the devil's soul-destroying will, and you thus bear testimony to your service to him.

Sin does to us what these demons did to this man they possessed—it twists and distorts, it degrades and destroys those who were created to glory in and enjoy the beauties of God. Think, for instance, of substance abuse and its effects in the lives of those who have sought those sinful pleasures of the body and mind. The streets of our cities are littered with the human wreckage of that sinful power, not at all unlike the man in this passage. What about pornography? Isn't this man a picture of how this sin, this device of the devil, works in those it captures? Solitude, a dirty nakedness, self-destructive restlessness.

Much the same could be said about racism or sexual promiscuity or addictions to gambling. These are all notorious though common sins. Perhaps you have avoided these. So what about pride? What about self-worship? They too lead to all that is pictured in this demon-wrecked man. A corporate headquarters can be just as much a graveyard of souls as is the adult video store.

Humanity, created in God's image for beauty and glory and fruitfulness, is degraded by sin, destroyed by the reign of the devil. So before moving on let's make one deliberate

DEMISE
DETERIORATION DESTRUCTION

application. This passage challenges us to understand that when we are toying with sin we are not getting away with a little fun. We are not indulging our freedom but our bondage; we are not finding what is real and pleasurable, but we are collaborating with the degradation and de-struction of our very selves. That is what is at stake with sin—not points gained or lost in some petty game, not sweets stolen from the jar, but the choice of death over life, for, as the apostle Paul put it, "the wages of sin is death" (Rom. 6:23).

Portrait of Christ's saving work

That is the first portrait in this passage, and the second stands in stark contrast. If the passage begins with the de-monic work to destroy this poor man, it centers on a second portrait, that of Christ's saving work to redeem and restore him. In particular we see two aspects of Christ's work, namely, its power and its redeeming purpose.

The demons were having quite their way with this man they had possessed. There they were in Gentile territory, presumably out of Jesus' way, having utterly overcome and dominated this man's personality and will. Therefore, when they saw the little boat with the small party landing, they raced down to attack, encountering them as soon as they stepped onto the shore. What they found there stopped them in their tracks, as Luke relates: "When he saw Jesus, he cried out and fell at his feet, shouting at the top of his voice, 'What do you want with me, Jesus, Son of the Most High God? I beg you, don't torture me!'" (8:28).

Three things draw our notice, the first of which is the demons' ability to recognize and identify Jesus for who he is. In the verse prior to our passage, the disciples responded

DEMONS RECOGNIZE WHO J. WAS

to Jesus' miracle of calming the winds and waves by asking, "Who is this?" The demons apparently knew the answer perfectly well. Notice particularly what they knew about him—not merely his name, Jesus, but also his identity as "Son of the Most High God." As we will see, they knew not only his person but also his office and authority. This gives us much insight as to how demons see Jesus and also reminds us that bare knowledge of Jesus as the Son of God does not necessarily convey salvation, which comes only through a faith these demons knew nothing of.

Second, we see Jesus' might, or power, over the demons. When they saw him, they immediately drove the possessed man to his knees and began groveling before the Lord. When Jesus asked for the man's name, the spokesman-demon replied, "Legion," to signify the great multitude of evil spirits involved. A Roman legion consisted of six thousand soldiers, although the word could be used to connote any multitude; we find from the size of the herd of pigs they entered that there were at least two thousand demons in this one man. And yet, even with such odds, two thousand demons to one Lord Jesus Christ, the demons did not even contemplate opposition. They immediately fell prostrate and began pleading. This man had no power in himself to oppose one demon, much less thousands, and neither do any of us, which is one reason why we should not focus on or direct our energies against demons. But what this man could not do, what we cannot do, Jesus can do easily by means of his divine and omnipotent power.

Third, we see Jesus' authority over the demons. Power is the ability to apply force; authority is the right to do so. Jesus evidently holds authority over the demons. "I beg you, don't torture me," the demon said. Luke 8:31 makes it obvious what this means, when the demons begged Jesus re-

POWER – force
AUTHORITY – right

peatedly "not to order them to go into the Abyss," that is, into hell. Matthew's Gospel supplies the additional detail that they reminded Jesus that it was not yet the appointed time for this, a clear reference to the final judgment that awaits the devil and all his minions at the end of days (8:29).

Seeing a large herd of pigs (Mark tells us there were about two thousand of them) the demons "begged Jesus to let them go into them, and he gave them permission." Luke continues, "When the demons came out of the man, they went into the pigs, and the herd rushed down the steep bank into the lake and was drowned" (8:32–33). Thus is seen Jesus' victory over the demons who so oppressed this man.

Before turning to the now-former demoniac, we may wonder why Jesus conceded to the demons' request. At least three reasons come to mind, the first of which is that it was true that the time had not yet come. Although he had come to crush the serpent's head, it was not yet the time when demonic activity was to be eradicated. This then was a means of delivering the man, who was worth a large herd of swine.

Second, Jesus must have noted the appropriateness of the pigs as a vessel for the demons. Under the law, swine were unclean, and by their plunging death into the sea Jesus prefigured the soon destruction of Satan and his followers in the lake of fire. Finally, Jesus may have wanted to give visible proof that the man was no longer possessed, while at the same time challenging the value system of the local people. Would they rejoice at the restoration of a man or lament the loss of their property?

If people are shocked at the means Jesus employed, the death of these creatures, they will be even more shocked to discover the ultimate means by which he overcame Satan and evil. That means was his own death, his own plunge into the Abyss, the marring of God's image in him, and his own alienation from heaven, all of which took place by means of the cross. The overthrow of evil and sin is costly. It must be so, and the cost of this herd of swine is nothing in comparison with the precious blood of Jesus that truly was the price of our redemption.

Humanity Restored

I said that this story portrays two aspects of Christ's saving work, the first of which is his power and authority. He came to oppose Satan's power and reign, to overcome him and plunder his house for the deliverance of Christ's own. But this passage shows something else about Jesus' saving work, namely, its purpose in the lives of those he redeems.

If our passage contrasts the work of demons with the work of Christ, that contrast is pointedly revealed in the transformation effected in this man. Luke tells us several things about him, beginning with the description that he was "sitting at Jesus' feet, dressed and in his right mind" (8:35). Here we have a portrait of true humanity restored by the saving work of Christ. One commentator, Darrell Bock, marks the change this way:

> In a complete reversal of the previously possessed man's demeanor, he is now clothed, whereas before he had been naked; he is now seated, whereas before he had been roaming; he is now associating with others as he sits at Jesus' feet, whereas before he sought solitude; he is now of sound mind,

whereas before he had been crying out in a loud voice; he is now comfortable in the presence of Jesus, whereas before he wanted nothing to do with him.[4]

Another commentator, William Lane, says, "The man whom neither chains nor men could restrain was sitting in a docile manner before Jesus; he who had terrified others as he ran naked among the tombs was now clothed; the one who had shrieked wildly and behaved violently was now fully recovered. So radical was the transformation that the townspeople were stunned and frightened."[5]

All that is what it means to be redeemed. So often, and rightly, we focus on what we have been delivered from—and we could understand this in the case of the once-demoniac. But notice how prominent is the description of what he has been saved to. He is saved to that for which he was created—the worship and enjoyment of God in Jesus Christ.

Let's look at these items one by one. First, this man is sitting at Jesus' feet, seeking to know him and learn of him. That is what true freedom is all about. The man is delivered from bondage but does not race off to the city, not to his old friends, not to the most convenient source of worldly pleasure. Instead he sits at the feet of Jesus and worships him.

No longer naked as in the past, the man is now clothed. Jesus has clothed him. Surely we are intended to think back to the scene in Genesis 3, after our first parents had fallen into sin, when God graciously clothed Adam and Eve. God sacrificed innocent animals in their place to cover their sinful condition; likewise this man is clothed by Jesus, just as all who are delivered by him are clothed by his righteousness. As the great hymn proclaims,

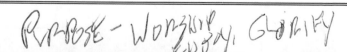

Jesus, thy blood and righteousness
　my beauty are, my glorious dress
'Midst flaming worlds, in these arrayed,
　with joy shall I lift up my head.

That is what it means to be clothed by Jesus Christ, no longer naked and exposed in our sin.

And then comes Luke's summative statement: "He was in his right mind." Not just that he was no longer insane, no longer howling and living like the demons that controlled him. That is true, but there is more. He has been delivered not just from raving lunacy but also to a right mind. He is worshiping the Lord; he wants to be with Jesus—that is what Luke tells us (8:38). Christ does the same for us— he gives us a right mind that no longer conforms to the pattern of this world, a mind that he renews day by day, with purity and joy and godly affections, as well as a heavenly appetite. He enables us to worship, which is what we were made for.

There is a question I often ask in pastoral situations, which is appropriate in this context now. Are you able to worship God? Can you sit in his presence, not restless but with peace and joy? Not seeking carnal excitement, but spiritually worshiping God on the basis of truth? It is there that our restless anxiety finds its cure, its resting place, and there alone, in the worship of the infinite God. We were made to worship God, and Christ's saving work is such as to restore the image of God in all who trust in him, giving us a sound and godly mind, which is no better seen than when we worship God through him. He enables us to live completely differently, with our hearts set on things above, not on things of the earth (Col. 3:2). If you have been delivered by him you know something about this already. If you will sit at his feet, if you will walk with him through this life, trusting him and his saving work, you will know more and more of this as you grow in his grace.

Portrait of Christ as Missionary Savior

The third portrait in this passage is of Christ as a missionary Savior. We see this both at the beginning and at the end of these verses.

What was Jesus doing in this Gentile region in the first place? Why was he in the midst of all this uncleanness, among tombs and herds of swine and demon-possessed madmen? The answer is that it was for this that he came into the world. For so it was written: "The people walking in darkness have seen a great light; on those living in the land of the shadow of death a light has dawned" (Isa. 9:2).

Jesus is a missionary Savior, and that means there is hope for you. We see this again and again in these miracle stories. There is no place he will not go, no one he will not touch. There is no corruption he will not cleanse. He touches the leper; he places his hand on those consumed by death; he stands with authority before the demon-possessed. He is therefore willing and able to save you, no matter your condition or where you are to be found. The only question is whether or not you will receive him as your Savior, whether you will trust him and proclaim him Lord.

How terrible to read of these local people, coming out to find their herd gone and the raving madman whole. Luke tells us how they responded to this great miracle: "They asked Jesus to leave them, because they were overcome with fear" (8:37). The reason for this is not quite clear in Luke's account, but in Mark we find that they asked Jesus to leave when they learned about their lost possessions. They were like many people are today, not wanting anyone or anything to interfere with the business of business, the accumulation of worldly things, of swine production and the like. They were indifferent to the restoration of this fellow human being and blind to the spiritual peril of their own souls.

What, we may ask, should they have done? They should have recognized that what happened to this demon-possessed man corresponded to their own need, just as it does to everyone apart from Christ. They should have realized all along that the demoniac was a picture of them in their sin. Seeing him from afar they should have thought, "I am like that, really. I am spending my days in a graveyard, a realm stalked by death and its finality, laboring for things that will perish." When they heard him howling and crying out by night, they should have said, "I am restless like that, kept awake by fear, by guilt, by unease, by emptiness, by an absence of purpose and peace." And then when they saw him clothed and peacefully seated, in his right mind before Jesus, they should have run to him as well, crying, "That man who was so much worse than I was is now so much better. What Jesus did for him I need done for me." But they were blind to all of this, and for the sake of their swine they turned away their only Savior.

It is the same for everyone. Many people weigh the claims of God's Word against the siren songs of this world, thinking, "I understand what is being said, but I fear Jesus will interfere with my worldly aspirations, with my designs for success, for money, glory, and pleasure." Anyone who thinks this way must understand that by turning Jesus away, by delaying their own submission to the Savior, they are forging the chains of their own bondage. In the next chapter of Luke's Gospel, with the picture of this restored man still lingering in our minds, Jesus sums up the reality facing us all with these words: "What good is it for a man to gain the whole world, and yet lose or forfeit his very self?" (Luke 9:25).

Many people think it will be easier to come to Jesus Christ after they have enjoyed the pleasures of sin for a while, after they have burrowed deeper into this world. In this they are greatly mistaken. It will not be easier but harder later on; you will be further down the broad lane that leads to destruction, longer and firmer in the grip of him who twists and corrupts men and women made in the image of God.

Though people turn away, it is not because Jesus lacks mercy and grace. That was not the case then. The man restored begged to follow Jesus, but where did Jesus send him? Back to his own people, back to his home, his old workplace, his family. "Tell how much God has done for you" (Luke 8:39), Jesus said to him, and the Gerasenes, even having rejected Jesus Christ, were not left without a witness. Such is his grace.

The man did what Jesus told him. He must have had a few awkward moments around the dinner table back home, just as everyone does who is redeemed and restored by Christ. But look at the last sentence in Luke 8:39: "So the man went away and told all over town how much Jesus had done for him." He didn't go around relating his intimate knowledge of demons, he didn't tell twisted tales of his past, he didn't glorify in what he had done in any way, but he spoke about Jesus Christ and what he had done. This man was very much in his right mind.

Jesus is a missionary Savior, and that means that we must be missionaries too. Like this man he delivered from possession, we have so much to tell about what Jesus has done for us. He has lived for us, he has died for us, and he has risen from the dead to be our living Lord and Savior forever. That is the final brush stroke in this portrait of humanity restored. From a living hell to a life of worship; from a life of alienation to fellowship with Jesus Christ. This is our own experience of salvation, from which we too gain a desire to tell everyone what he has done for us.

8

Tears and Laughter

Luke 8:40–56

They laughed at him, knowing that she was dead.
But he took her by the hand and said, "My child, get up!"
Her spirit returned, and at once she stood up. Then Jesus
told them to give her something to eat. Her parents
were astonished, but he ordered them not to tell
anyone what had happened. (LUKE 8:53–57)

When you are studying the miracles of Jesus, one thing you are sure to notice is the sheer enormity of suffering in the world. These accounts have offered a cavalcade of misery and torment and hardship. In our studies so far we have encountered the sick, the diseased, the lame, the possessed, and the dead. We have seen the full range of emotional and spiritual suffering: fear, loneliness, insanity, unspeakable grief and loss. All of this, as we have often observed, traces its origin to the entry of sin into the world. How heavily it all must have weighed upon our Lord Jesus; no wonder he often withdrew to unburden himself upon his heavenly Father.

As we move forward in Luke 8, we find more of the same. We meet a father who is brought to his knees by the life-threatening illness of his beloved daughter. We encounter a woman who for twelve long years has suffered from a medical affliction that not only troubled her body but also made her a social and spiritual recluse. We come to a house where mourners wail in tears and laugh in derision at the idea of a savior. In the middle of it all is the Lord Jesus Christ. In each case he lifts up the downtrodden, gives hope to the destitute, turns tears of sorrow into tears of joy, the laughter of scorn into grateful cries of joy.

No Hopeless Cases

It is noteworthy that this passage occurs toward the end of a major section of Luke's Gospel. There are four major sections in Luke: the introductory chapters, followed by Jesus' public ministry in Galilee and the nearby Gentile regions, as he assembled his twelve disciples. At the end of Luke 9 he begins his travels toward Jerusalem, and the focus narrows to the training of those disciples. Finally, beginning in Luke 19 we have the Passion Week, which culminates in Jesus' death and resurrection.

The particular miracle we are considering occurs toward the end of the second of these sections—Jesus' public ministry around the Sea of Galilee, a ministry heavily laced with teaching in parables and miraculous works. The intent of this phase of his ministry was to declare the coming of God's kingdom and to gather his disciples.

The period leading up to this miracle was a momentous one. Jesus has been doing things like healing the centurion's servant and resurrecting the widow of Nain's dead son. In the middle of these records comes the parable of the sower, in which Jesus challenges the people to a faith that takes root, and not a fleeting faith or a mere worldly interest in his affairs. After this he withdrew across the lake, calming the storm along the way and delivering the famous demoniac on the far shore. It is no surprise then that Luke tells us that when Jesus returned from this venture, "a crowd welcomed him, because they were all expecting him" (8:40). Particularly in an era without many entertainment options, this was a big-time attraction, and the people flocked to see Jesus.

Apparently it was to Capernaum that Jesus returned, which was the scene of several prior miracles. Matthew's Gospel tells us that a delegation from John the Baptist met him, inquiring about Jesus' ministry (9:14–17). While that was going on, a man named Jairus appeared, having undoubtedly seen many of Jesus' prior miracles and being in dire need of Jesus' help. Luke tells us, "A man named Jairus, a ruler of the synagogue, came and fell at Jesus' feet, pleading with him to come to his house because his only daughter, a girl of about twelve, was dying" (8:41–42).

As Jesus was on his way to this man's house, however, the crowd pressed close around him, obviously wanting to see what new wonder Jesus was engaged in. Luke tells us they practically crushed him. Among them was a woman with a desperate need, and she literally reached out to Jesus for help.

These are the two main figures in this story, and they could hardly be more different. The man was a ruler of the synagogue, which meant that he was in charge of the worship service, with the reading of the Scriptures and the teaching of the commandments. Obviously he was a person of high social and religious standing in the community.

The woman was on the opposite end of the scale. Luke says this about her: "A woman was there who had been subject to bleeding for twelve years, but no one could heal her" (8:43). This probably points to a uterine hemorrhage, a condition that not only brought discomfort but also rendered her ceremonially unclean under the law. Furthermore, should she touch anyone else, that person also became unclean, so her condition made her a social pariah (see Lev. 15:19).

It seems clear that Luke wants us to compare these two figures. One is a synagogue ruler; the other is barred from the place of worship. One has a twelve year-old daughter he loves; the other has been an outcast that very length of time. One is prosperous and the other destitute. Both were desperate in their need and yet inhibited from approaching Jesus. Despite all their differences, they had this in common—only Jesus could help them. They both came to him and were gladly received by him.

This contrast brings to light the first point I want to make, which is that there are no hopeless cases when it comes to Jesus Christ. Both of these people are poor prospects for salvation through Jesus, and yet both are able to trust him and be blessed.

First, the synagogue ruler falls into a class of persons who were hardly distinguished for their humility and faith in response to Jesus' ministry. So far in Luke's Gospel much has happened in synagogues. It was in the synagogue at Nazareth, his hometown, that Jesus announced his public ministry as fulfilling the messianic prophecies. The result was that they tried to stone him and drive him over a cliff

(Luke 4:16–17). Later, in the synagogue of Capernaum— perhaps the very one over which this man was ruler—Jesus encountered and delivered a demon-possessed man (4:33–34). Later yet, in this or a nearby synagogue, Jesus healed a man with a shriveled hand. The Pharisees and other leaders pounced on this to accuse Jesus of violating the law against working on the Sabbath (6:6–7). As a group, the religious establishment, men like Jairus, was intimidated by Jesus. He threatened their privileged status, and they vehemently opposed him. Ultimately it was such men who crucified him.

Yet here we have this synagogue ruler bowing at Jesus' feet, beseeching his aid. How easy it would have been for him to say, "Others can come to Jesus, but I cannot. I cannot sacrifice my pride and bow before this rabbi my fellow leaders despise. I cannot lower myself to the kind of thing others freely do. It is hopeless for me." But that is not what he said. Why? Because he loved his daughter and she was dying. He understood that Jesus had power to save, so he cast aside his petty objections and came to Jesus. He put aside his pride and envy, his standing in the community, and turned to Jesus with faith, bowing before him. Because of his faith, Jesus received him.

Quite in contrast is this woman who was not merely low on the social scale—she wasn't even allowed on it. If the synagogue ruler might have been kept away by his pride and self-sufficiency, she might have been kept back by her lowliness and despair. She had suffered this bleeding for twelve years. Luke, who was a physician, tells us she could find no help anywhere. Not only was her medical condition hopeless, but also she was kept back from human society by the ceremonial law regarding impurity. Her coming through this crowd would make numerous people unclean by her touch, so she had no access to the Great Healer who was passing by. We can imagine Jesus walking close by to where she sat, just close enough for her to lean out and touch his hem, believing he could heal her.

There she is reaching out just to touch the hem of Jesus' robe. She might well have said, "I see why others go to Jesus, but it is no use for me. I have tried other healers, and they declared my case hopeless. What is more, I am relegated to the alleys by my lot in life and cannot venture out to where Jesus is. It may be possible for others, but it is hopeless for me." But that is not what she said. She overcame her reluctance and hoped once more, venturing out to come to Jesus Christ.

Together these two tell us there are no hopeless cases. If you are rich, that is no barrier to your salvation. I know that the wealthy and the educated portray Christianity as a crutch for the ignorant and poor and weak. It may not go over well with your set for you to attend a Bible-preaching church. You may raise eyebrows at the country club if you submit yourself to Christ, but if you feel your need for salvation, yours is not a hopeless case. You may come to Jesus, and he will receive you gladly.

The same is true if you are poor, if you can't afford fine clothes, if you are not well read and have no religious friends. These are the kinds of excuses people make to avoid church, to not worship God, and to relegate themselves to unbelief and alienation from the Lord. While the scholars say, "Christianity is for the ignorant," the uneducated say, "Christianity is for the high and learned." How easy it is to say that Jesus is for someone else, that it is hopeless in your case. But there are no hopeless cases. There are none Christ rejects if you will come to him. Indeed, he is the Savior of all the hopeless.

The Necessity of Faith

The encounter with this woman brings to light our second point, which is that Christ's saving power demands faith. In order to benefit from the salvation he offers, we must trust in him, which is what we see in this woman. Hers is an instructive example, and I want to point out six things about her faith.

First, it was awareness of her need that brought her to Jesus. We have already discussed her plight, her issue of blood with the social and religious implications. Luke tells us no one had been able to help her. To this, Mark's Gospel adds that "she had suffered a great deal under the care of many doctors and had spent all she had, yet instead of getting better she grew worse" (5:26). This is what brought her to Jesus Christ, her great and desperate need. The same is true for everyone who comes to Jesus. They come because they know their need. They know they are filthy, they are sick of soul, they are downcast in spirit, they are guilty of sin.

If you are not much interested in Jesus, if you see little reason to draw near to him and to be associated with him publicly, a likely reason is that you do not feel your need. You do not know yourself to be a sinner, to have a great and mortal sickness of spirit; you do not recognize that your life is being wasted and misspent; you do not contemplate the righteousness and justice of God that must condemn you in your sins.

That is why we preach the law of God, because there we see our sinfulness, like a mirror that shows the dirt upon our face. That is why we proclaim what Paul wrote in Romans 3:23: "For all have sinned and fall short of the glory of God." That is why we go on to what Paul said in Romans 6:23, that "the wages of sin is death." What brings you to Jesus is comprehension of your need. J. C. Ryle wrote:

> He that desires to be saved . . . let him know this day that the first steps towards heaven are a deep sense of sin and a lowly estimate of ourselves. Let him cast away that weak and silly tradition that the beginning of religion is to feel ourselves "good." Let him rather grasp that grand scriptural principle, that we must begin by feeling "bad" and that, until we really feel "bad" we know nothing of true goodness or saving Christianity. Happy is he who has learned to draw near to God with the prayer of the publican: "God be merciful to me a sinner" (Lk. 18:13).[1]

That, of course, was Jesus' teaching in the Sermon on the Mount, which began with these words: "Blessed are the poor in spirit, for theirs is the kingdom of heaven" (Matt. 5:3). Awareness of our need brings us to Jesus.

Second, this woman came having tried many false remedies before. She had been to many physicians, and they had afflicted her while taking all her money. I just observed that many people shun Jesus because they do not feel their need. But there are others—I believe a great many in our day—who do know their need, who recognize that they are lost, who do feel dirty and broken and vulnerable but are looking for answers in all the wrong places.

Perhaps you are like that. You have felt your emptiness, your sense of alienation that results from separation from God because of sin. But what have you done? You have pursued pleasure or success, you have given yourself into the hands of the entertainment industry, you have tried therapies or have tried to do good works. Yet you find your soul not better off but worse. Again Ryle addresses this well:

> The state of many a lost sinner's heart is set before us in this description . . . who have felt their sins deeply and have been deeply troubled that they are not forgiven and not ready to die. They seek consolation but do not know where to look. They have tried false remedies and only find themselves getting worse. They have tired themselves out with every conceivable man-made device for obtaining spiritual health. But all has been in vain. In short, like this woman, they are ready to say, "There is no hope for me. I shall never be saved."[2]

But third, when she came upon Jesus, she believed he had the power to heal her. Mark tells us what happened with a bit more detail here than Luke. "When she heard about Jesus, she came up behind him in the crowd and touched his cloak, because she thought, 'If I just touch his clothes, I will be healed.' Immediately her bleeding stopped and she felt in her body that she was freed from her suffering" (Mark 5:27–28). Here we see what faith is, namely, relying on the power of Jesus for our own salvation, trusting his saving work for our redemption.

Surely when this woman saw Jesus, she remembered the accounts of his great miracles and hope sprang up within her. Here was One who had power far beyond that of the physicians she had seen. He could cure the leper and raise the dead. With faith drawn from what he had done, she resolved just to touch the Great Physician and believe, and she was healed. The key to this was her faith, as Jesus commented: "Daughter, your faith has healed you" (Luke 8:48).

That is what all of us must do. It is not that our faith itself has any power, but that Jesus has power to save us, to heal our soul and cleanse away our sins. By faith we lay hold of him and his power to save. This woman had heard about Jesus and so she came; that same good news comes to us now through God's Word. And where every human remedy fails he is still the Great Healer; if you will reach out to him with faith, you will find that he is able and willing to save.

Fourth, there is the quality of her faith. There is much to commend, as Jesus does, about her faith. There was a boldness in what this woman did. But there is also a certain timidity. She dared not come openly, as Jairus had done; she dared not lay hold of Jesus firmly, but merely touched the very hem of his garment. I do not say this to fault her in any way, but surely in her own eyes her faith had seemed weak and imperfect.

Many people feel the same way, and this woman reminds us that what matters is not the strength of our faith but the object of our faith. A weak faith may receive a strong Christ; imperfect belief lays hold of a perfect Savior. Therefore no one should be discouraged by the weakness of his faith but rather emboldened by the power of the Savior to whom our faith clings.

Fifth, Jesus required this woman to give testimony to what had happened to her. "Who touched me?" he asked (Luke 8:45). Peter, apparently thinking that Jesus had lost his wits, responded that all the people were pressing in on them. Surely all of them had touched him!

> But Jesus said, "Someone touched me; I know that power has gone out from me." Then the woman, seeing that she could not go unnoticed, came trembling and fell at his feet. In the presence of all the

people, she told why she had touched him and how she had been instantly healed. Then he said to her, "Daughter, your faith has healed you. Go in peace." (Luke 8:46–48)

We are not told exactly why she was trying to slip away, but the reason is not difficult to sort out. She was unused to attention and probably reluctant to share the details of her situation before such a crowd. She may well have feared a reproof for touching Jesus while she was still unclean, even though her defilement was no match for his purity. Jesus, however, felt the power go out from him. That is not some expression of magic but rather his awareness of his healing power going forth in response to faith.

Jesus' action shows us that he does not allow salvation to involve only an impersonal encounter, a fleeting brush with his grace that leaves no lasting mark. Jesus knows his own and sees the heart that reaches out to him; he can, as one pastor put it, "tell the fingers of faith from the elbows of unbelief." So he called out, "Who touched me?" The woman, realizing she could not escape him, came back trembling, fell at Jesus' feet, and explained everything before the eyes and ears of the great throng.

Many believers try to do what she did. They want to benefit from Jesus without public exposure, but it is not possible. If you try to be a secret Christian, rest assured that Christ will insist that you come back into the light of day, for it is the purpose of our salvation that we give glory to God through him. Psalm 50:15 says, "Call upon me in the day of trouble; I will deliver you, and you will honor me." As Paul says in Romans 10, confessing Jesus with your mouth is a necessary part of true and saving faith. Jesus did not let this woman depart without completing what she had begun by faith.

Finally, sixth, her faith gained her not only healing but also peace. I realize that people do come to Jesus for something other than forgiveness of their sin and reconciliation to God. This woman came for physical healing, and people today come for the same, for illumination, for some sort of magical power having nothing to do with God himself. Jesus goes out of his way to make sure no such thing will happen here. Looking at this woman with the great compassion displayed in all his miracles, he said, "Daughter, your faith has healed you. Go in peace."

She got more than she bargained for, not merely her health but her restoration as a person, the gift of peace from God incarnate. Only by faith in him, not by religious observances, not by good works, but only from a trusting relationship with Jesus Christ will we find such restoration, inner rest, and peace.

Faith Must Overcome Obstacles

The story does not end there, for as this encounter drew to a close, messengers came from Jairus's house. Luke tells us, "While Jesus was still speaking, someone came from the house of Jairus, the synagogue ruler. 'Your daughter is dead,' he said. 'Don't bother the teacher any more.' Hearing this, Jesus said to Jairus, "'Don't be afraid; just believe, and she will be healed'" (8:49–50).

This produces our third main point from this passage, namely, that faith must overcome obstacles. The key statement here comes from Jesus: "Don't be afraid; just believe."

"Do not be afraid! Fear not!" These are among the most repeated phrases in the Bible, and they are always spoken when faith collides with the appearance of certain danger or failure or death. This is what God said to Abraham when he told him to wander as a pilgrim throughout the land of promise. "Do not be afraid, Abram; I am your shield, your very great reward" (Gen. 15:1 paraphrase). That is what Moses said to the people of Israel when they were backed up against the Red Sea with Pharaoh's army bearing down. "Do not be afraid. Stand firm and you will see the deliverance the LORD will bring" (Ex. 14:13). It is what the angel said to Mary when she learned that she would bear a virgin-born child, the Son of the Most High God (Luke 1:30); what Peter counseled to the church facing persecution: "'Do not fear what they fear; do not be frightened.' But in your hearts set apart Christ as Lord" (1 Peter 3:14–15). Always, where the gospel is believed, fear is pushed away, like sunlight breaking through dark clouds.

The fact, however, that Jesus said these words to Jairus indicates that there were reasons for him to doubt and be afraid. The first of these was the evidence itself. Jairus had sought out Jesus when things were already dire. Luke 8:42 tells us that his daughter "was dying" when he came. All the commotion regarding this woman who was healed had delayed Jesus, which must have worried him, and then came this messenger, saying, "Don't bother the teacher. She has died." All the evidence pointed now to a hopeless situation, and these words must have torn Jairus's heart. This accounts for Jesus' encouragement: "Don't be afraid; just believe, and she will be healed."

The other source of fear and doubt was the unbelief of others. This started with the messenger but only intensified as they drew near to his home, where "all the people were wailing and mourning for her" (Luke 8:52). In ancient Israel, professional mourners were employed, and a man of this prominence must have attracted a good many, people who would wail and lament and beat their breasts. This is

what he encountered when they arrived, the mourners having already come and begun their labor. How this must
have disheartened the synagogue ruler. Jesus, however, said
to them, "Stop wailing. . . . She is not dead but asleep." At
this the mourners laughed, scoffing at Jesus' statement, for
they had seen the dead girl. Their unbelief must have been
a great barrier to the faith of Jairus.

It is the same for us in our trials and struggles. I admit
that the evidence seems stacked against our faith. It seems
that what works in this life is money and power and fame.
It looks as if the way of sin and deceit and pleasure is the
way to be happy. The forces arrayed against us—the world,
the flesh, and the devil—are much too strong for us. I admit that. The accumulation of that evidence and more ar-
gues for doubt and unbelief and fear.

Furthermore, all around us is the unbelief of others, the
scoffing of those who think Christianity is a ridiculous
crutch, its teaching unenlightened lunacy. You tell co-
workers that you are trusting God, and they roll their eyes.
They snicker at your claim that God is watching over you.
You have family members who tell you to face the realities
of being on your own in this world. The media and the
schools and the government conspire to present a bleak
picture alleviated only by temporary pleasure and stoic res-
ignation. All this unbelief and doubt presses against us as
an obstacle to our faith.

It is worth noting that Luke 8 begins with the parable
of the sower, which is meant to influence how we read
these stories that come right afterward. Jesus spoke of seeds
that fell along the path where the ground was hard, representing those who do not believe. Other seed fell on rock
and withered for lack of moisture, signifying those who "receive the word with joy . . . but . . . have no root" (8:13).

Yet other seeds fell among thorns and were choked out. These, he said, are "those who hear, but . . . are choked by life's worries, riches and pleasures" (v. 14). Standing against those bad examples is the seed that fell on good soil, which yielded an abundant crop. Jesus said, "The seed on good soil stands for those with a noble and good heart, who hear the word, retain it, and by persevering produce a crop" (v. 15).

That was exactly the kind of challenge facing Jairus. Would he succumb to fear and unbelief, to the apparent evidence and to the cynical attitude of all those around him? Against all those reasons for fear and doubt was stacked just one thing: the power of Jesus Christ to save. Jairus knew something about that. Here was evidence that the unbelievers had failed to account for. Jairus had presumably seen Christ's power demonstrated at the synagogue and had heard the reports all around the region of what Jesus was doing. Just now and right before his eyes he had heard testimony from the woman who had suffered from the bleeding condition; perhaps it was for Jairus's sake that Jesus had brought about her testimony. Against all the other evidence of hopelessness, Jairus believed, he kept his heart because Jesus was there with him, and Jesus had power to save. Jesus is the One who can say in the face of such a hopeless scene, "Fear not; just believe."

Jairus's faith is not explicitly mentioned in the text, but Jesus' action makes clear that he did believe. "Just believe, and she will be healed," Jesus said, and healed she was.

Jesus told the mourners the girl was only asleep. Some commentators have used this to indicate that she had not died but only fallen into a coma. But that was not Jesus' point; his point was that her spirit had not gone beyond his reach. With regard to what he would do, this was not death but the falling into a temporary sleep. Luke tells us what happened: "He took her by the hand and said, 'My child, get up!' Her spirit returned, and at once she stood up. Then Jesus told them to give her something to eat. Her parents were astonished, but he ordered them not to tell anyone what had happened" (8:54–56).

Tears and Laughter

Two points of interest close this account. First, Jesus directed the parents to feed the girl. This both indicates his comprehensive interest and proves that this was no apparition he had raised. Second, he "ordered them not to tell anyone what had happened." This is in contrast with what he commanded to the demoniac he had delivered over in the Gentile lands. I think the best explanation is that Jesus wanted to curtail the growing tendency to associate his ministry simply with the power to give people what they wanted. Darrell Bock explains, "Jesus knows that he is headed for a different kind of ministry than people will want from him. . . . The type of commitment that will be required of them, should they follow him, is one of suffering, not comfort."[3]

This passage concludes a great chapter of miracles, mighty works that declare Christ's power over winds and waves, over demons and sickness and finally even death. Jesus is the Savior who can meet our every need, if we will look to him in faith. His power and compassion are a great encouragement to press on in faith despite every obstacle, despite all the testimony of the world, all the contrary evidence that begs us to doubt.

This eighth chapter of Luke's Gospel, beginning with the parable of the sower, is about faith in Christ, and the story of Jairus and the woman are the exclamation point emphasizing its centrality. First, we saw there is no hopeless cause when Christ is near. Second, they each show us that Christ's power demands faith as the response. Then, through Jairus we see that faith must overcome all obstacles. Finally, at the end we find one last encouragement, the lesson that overcoming faith receives a great reward.

Great is the reward of faith in Jesus Christ, because through faith we receive his saving power. At the end of the passage that power is wonderfully seen in the transformation of the tears and laughter. Amid tears of pain and loss Jesus arrives with power to save—and those cries are transformed into tears of joy. When he spoke about the girl waking up, there was laughter, the laughter of unbelief and derision, but when he had shown his compassion and power it was only the laughter of relief, the laughter of astonished delight that came from the mother and the father. The presence of Jesus Christ changes everything, even the tears and laughter in the house of this man who trusted him.

I said at the beginning of this chapter that the miracles of Jesus show us something of the misery and suffering of this world. Try though we might, we will not escape the kinds of things we see in these passages. Debilitating illness, oppression from spiritual enemies, the danger of life in a changing and threatening world, the specter of our own death, and mourning for the loss of those who are dear to us. It is in the midst of these and other trials, it is in the presence of darkness and pain and fear that we are tested like this synagogue ruler was tested. "Fear not, only believe," Jesus says. If we will, not just when the discussion is abstract and safe but when the walls of our lives seem to be tumbling down, then we will know the reality of his power and peace.

Sickness and sorrow would come again to Jairus's house. This girl, I fully trust, did ultimately die. That is not the point. The point is that overcoming faith receives the presence of Jesus Christ and the power of his life. This miracle does not guarantee that none will grow sick, that none of us will die—we will know sickness, and should Christ tarry we all will die, and soon enough. Rather, like all the miracles, it is a window into the day to come, into the kingdom Christ brings, when death will reign no more. On that day, as Scripture promises, "They will be his people, and God himself will be with them and be their God. He will wipe every tear from their eyes. There will be no more death or mourning or crying or pain, for the old order of things has passed away" (Rev. 21:3–4).

Only believe, and do not be afraid.

Feeding the
Five Thousand

Luke 9:12–17

Taking the five loaves and the two fish and looking up to heaven, he gave thanks and broke them. Then he gave them to the disciples to set before the people. They all ate and were satisfied, and the disciples picked up twelve basketfuls of broken pieces that were left over. (LUKE 9:16–17)

All of the miracles we have examined so far in our studies took place during Jesus' Galilean ministry. That was a period of very public proclamation of the kingdom of God, along with the miracles that accompanied the teaching. We come now to the culmination of this phase of ministry as Luke presents it, to a miracle that drew together everything Jesus had been doing in this Galilean period. Immediately afterward comes Peter's great confession of Christ and then the transfiguration, which together end this early phase and mark a major transition in Jesus' earthly ministry. From here he leaves Galilee, traveling through Perea and Judea on the way to Jerusalem and ultimately the cross.

The feeding of the five thousand therefore took place at a crossroads in Jesus' ministry, and it was one of Jesus' most significant miracles. It is exceptional for the clarity with which it reveals his identity as the Son of God and seems to have had a major impact in leading Peter to his profession of faith. Furthermore, when we compare the various Gospels, we find that this is the only miracle that occurs in all four. This important account hooks into deep theological strands that speak volumes about Jesus and his ministry, and therefore this miracle was accorded special importance in the biblical records about our Lord.

Miracle or Moral?

One other thing makes this a great miracle, and that is the way it confounds those who want to deny the miraculous or supernatural in the Gospels. This was a pet project of liberal theology in the nineteenth and twentieth centuries, but it is still with us by means of groups like the Jesus Seminar, which are looking for the so-called real and historical Jesus lurking behind the biblical record.

Liberal theology is able to get at the historical reality, that is, the naturalistic and nonmiraculous reality, behind the biblical accounts by means of reinterpretation. The main tactic is to see the miracle accounts as pointing to a moral or ethical breakthrough rather than a genuine supernatural intrusion. In this passage such reinterpretation looks something like this: Jesus didn't feed five thousand people with five loaves and two fish—such a belief is preposterous, they would say. No, his example of faith inspired others to break out the food they had been stashing away for themselves. It was a miracle of generosity, not of divine multiplication. It challenges us to open our own secret caches and joyfully share with those in need. It does not call for us to believe in Jesus' divinity but to donate to the local food bank.

That sounds nice, but there are problems. Indeed, there are such major problems that I think this is one of the best miracle accounts for refuting this kind of teaching. First, it is noteworthy that not one of the four Gospel writers either noticed or recorded anything like this reinterpretation. All of them—and we have four independent sources, two of whom were eyewitnesses and participants—seem to have thought it was a genuine miracle. Second, remember that three of the four Gospels were written at a time when a great number of eyewitnesses would still have been living. Only John came significantly later. Obviously Matthew, Mark, and Luke felt comfortable making the claim that Jesus performed this miracle just as they said, while knowing that many eyewitnesses could sustain or refute whatever they wrote. Either they were lying in the face of all these eyewitnesses or this was a great miracle just as they described.

Finally, when we study this miracle account in context, it is impossible to believe that the liberal version could produce the kind of effects the Gospels record. Luke's Gospel directly links this miracle to Peter's belief that Jesus is the Christ sent from God (9:20). In John's Gospel, the people connected this miracle to the manna God provided during the time of Moses. They exclaimed, "Surely this is the Prophet who is to come into the world" (John 6:14). The miraculous in the Gospels is not an easily explained anachronism but is essential to the whole flow of these inspired accounts of Jesus' life and ministry. They are so essential that without them we get a different Jesus and a different gospel altogether.

A Sign of Jesus' Deity

If this passage of Scripture did nothing but confound unbelieving and liberal theology it would greatly glorify God and serve a great purpose. But it has much more to offer us, beginning with this: it is a sign of Jesus' deity. A sign points to something else. It identifies something or someone, and this miracle identifies Jesus as the Son of God.

The passage begins with Jesus gathering the Twelve for some rest and recuperation. They had just been through a busy time, as the opening verses of Luke 9 inform us. Jesus had sent them out across the land in groups of two to preach the kingdom of God, to cure and drive out demons in his name (9:1–2). During this time John the Baptist was so recklessly put to death by King Herod, who then seems to have turned his attention to Jesus and his following. Apparently Jesus withdrew his disciples outside of Herod's jurisdiction in order to protect them and to avoid a premature confrontation.

The crowds, however, drawn by all that Jesus had done, went with them. Luke tells us, "He welcomed them and spoke to them about the kingdom of God, and healed those who needed healing" (9:11). Toward the end of the day the disciples came to Jesus and said, "Send the crowd away so they can go to the surrounding villages and countryside and find food and lodging, because we are in a remote place here" (v. 12). There seems to be some callous disregard for the mass of people, but also a practical view regarding how best to handle the situation. Jesus' reply must have stunned them, for he said, "You give them something to eat" (v. 13). Astonished and bewildered, they answered him, "'We have only five loaves of bread and two fish—unless we go and buy food for all this crowd.' (About five thousand men were there.)." Jesus took that small amount of food, five pieces of bread with two small fish (the precise description identifies them as something like sardines), and he fed the whole great multitude, five thousand male adults, not to mention the women and children who would have swelled that number dramatically.

This miracle plainly reveals Jesus' divinity, that is, his identity as the Son of God. Who else could so multiply nature's provision but the One who is the Lord of nature, the Creator himself, God incarnate? In performing this particular miracle, Jesus recalls the reader of the Old Testament to other outstanding miracles in which hungry people were fed by the power of God. The prophet Elisha had done this, feeding one hundred men with only twenty loaves (2 Kings 4:42–44). More memorable is the feeding of the nation of Israel in the wilderness with manna from heaven. Moses had delivered them from the bondage in Egypt, and God had fed them in the desert. Here, the God who gave manna in the desert, who fed Elijah beside the brook, who fed the hundred through the hand of Elisha, now gives this people their daily bread by the power of his own divine hand. Jesus had been teaching about the kingdom of God, Luke tells us, and what a demonstration of that kingdom this is!

At the end of his Gospel the apostle John says that these things were written so "that you may believe that Jesus is the Christ, the Son of God, and that by believing you may have life in his name" (20:31). In all of his life on this earth, there were few stronger manifestations to the deity of Jesus Christ than this feeding of the five thousand.

One of the things we always want to look for when studying the Bible is what the passage tells us about God. This particular passage not only tells us that Jesus is God but also shows us very much about what God is like. Jesus would later say, "Anyone who has seen me has seen the Father" (John 14:9), and in this miracle he displays several marvelous facets of God's holy character. We see his compassion as he cared for the needs and troubles of this many people. We see his zeal for God's people, rousing himself from weariness in order to meet their need. Jesus was ready to be inconvenienced for them as he is for us. When we compare this scene with what we see of King Herod in the passage immediately beforehand, we see Jesus' meekness of heart. He did not sup from silver platters with fawning courtiers, but he ate plain bread with the poor. The Lord loves to dwell with the lowly and the meek. He came not to be served but to serve and to give his life a ransom for many (Matt. 20:28). Finally, and most obviously, Jesus here demonstrates the power of God. He is armed with might so that no need is too difficult for him to fulfill. Compassionate, zealous to serve, lowly of heart, mighty in power—that is the God Jesus Christ reveals to the world.

The Exodus in Microcosm

The second great point presented by this passage has to do with Jesus' ministry, indeed, with the nature of Christian salvation. I stated that this particular miracle culminates a whole period of Jesus' career. In fact, what took place there summarizes the whole of his ministry and saving work. It achieves this by presenting Jesus' ministry as the Exodus in microcosm.

The greatest redemptive event of the Bible until the coming of Christ was the Exodus. It was then that the nation of Israel was formed, having been delivered from the house of bondage in Egypt by the power of God. Moses led them out of Egypt, through the wilderness for forty years, and ultimately he sent them into the land of promise. All through the New Testament that is seen as a model for what salvation in Jesus Christ is all about, nowhere more dramatically than in this passage.

The first clue to this comes in Luke's version, which describes the location as a desert. This occurs in Luke 9:12, where the New International Version renders it as "in a remote place." The Greek word here is "desert." This is puzzling at first, because John tells us "there was plenty of grass in that place" (John 6:10), which hardly describes a desert. You see how the New International Version tries to resolve this, taking Luke's meaning to be an out-of-the-way or remote locale. But instead of an error or even an exaggeration on Luke's part, it seems clear that he is making a deliberate allusion to the Exodus, when Moses led Israel out of bondage into the desert to meet with God.

Another clue comes from John's account, which informs us that the Passover feast was near (6:4). The point of this is not chronology but theology. The Passover was the great Jewish feast that celebrated the Exodus, and at this time of the year the people were supposed to go to Jerusalem to come before the Lord. These people had gone to the Lord, but they had not gone to Jerusalem—they had gone to Jesus. Here they were before the Lord Jesus Christ, where the kingdom of God is proclaimed and revealed, receiving from him the true Passover feast.

We see how this therefore culminates Jesus' Galilean ministry. In the Exodus, Moses delivered the people from bondage to Pharaoh by means of great miracles, just as Jesus here had been delivering them from Satan's reign, that is, from demons and sickness and even death. The culmination of Moses' work was the Passover, when God sent his avenger to strike down all the firstborn of Egypt. Only the Israelites, who had feasted upon the lamb and then spread its blood upon their door, were spared the wrath of God. The Passover meal was to be eaten by those ready for travel, pilgrims on their way. Exodus 12:11 told them, "This is how you are to eat it: with your cloak tucked into your belt, your sandals on your feet and your staff in your hand." Here, along the shores of the Sea of Galilee, those who had seen Jesus' miracles, who had heard his teaching, now gathered around him as pilgrims on their journey, with staff in hand, and they were called to believe on him as the true Lamb of God, the true Passover Lamb sacrificed for them.

The Exodus picture is made complete as Jesus had the people sit down in their various divisions. Just as Moses led the tribes out, gathered by their divisions in tribes and clans and families, Jesus tells the disciples, "Have them sit down in groups of about fifty each." Israel's tribes were organized with the tabernacle of the Lord in the center; so also is it here. We are reminded of John's statement that in Jesus Christ, "the Word became flesh and made his tabernacle among us" (John 1:14). And there God himself fed them with manna from heaven, even as Jesus Christ multiplied these loaves.

It is for all those reasons that I describe this miracle account as the Exodus in microcosm. The new Israel are those gathered around Jesus Christ, who feeds them in their desert journey, who reveals God's glory as did the Shekinah glory cloud of old. Here is the true Passover feast at which

Jesus Christ is both Lord and host. But the great reality that is pressed forth, the central feature of this picture, is this: he is the Lamb, and his is the blood that causes God's wrath to pass over.

That is the central message of this miracle, as Jesus makes so clear in the entire sixth chapter of John. What was Jesus getting at when he fed all these hungry people? Here is what Jesus himself said:

> I am the bread of life. He who comes to me will never go hungry, and he who believes in me will never be thirsty. . . . Here is the bread that comes down from heaven, which a man may eat and not die. I am the living bread that came down from heaven. If anyone eats of this bread, he will live forever. This bread is my flesh, which I will give for the life of the world. (John 6:35, 50–51)

This is not about how to feed the poor, much less about eating a wafer after a priest has spoken a few lines of Latin over it. Jesus is referring to a relationship with him, to faith in him and in his work. "He who comes to me will never go hungry, and he who believes in me will never be thirsty." That is what this is about, coming to Jesus and believing on him, so that people dead in their sins might have life, everlasting life. That is the hunger of which he spoke and the food he had in mind. "I am the bread of life," he said. "This is the bread that came down from heaven. Your forefathers ate manna and died, but he who feeds on this bread will live forever" (John 6:58). Jesus is, as John the Baptist foretold, "the Lamb of God, who takes away the sin of the world" (John 1:29).

Yes, this miracle urges us to have compassion on the

hungry and lost. Yes, it rebukes us if we are greedy and unwilling to share with others. Yes, it finds its reflection in the sacrament of the Lord's Supper, which came afterward and finds its significance here—not the other way around. All those things are true only after we have come as hungry sinners to the Bread of Life, to the Lamb who was slain, and feed upon him unto forgiveness and life eternal, until we come to him and believe on his name and are saved. "I tell you the truth," he says, "unless you eat the flesh of the Son of Man and drink his blood, you have no life in you. Whoever eats my flesh and drinks my blood has eternal life, and I will raise him up at the last day" (John 6:54). This is the great Passover feast, and he is the Lamb.

What then does it mean to be a follower of Jesus? This Exodus picture answers the question. It is to come with staff in hand, with your cloak tucked into your belt, a pilgrim departing from the land of bondage and headed toward your home in the land of promise. It is the kingdom of God in this desert world, the Exodus people saved by the blood of the Lamb, fed by the Lord, led by the Lord, to the place of rest that is far ahead.

Does that sound a wearisome, unattractive prospect, to follow Jesus as an alien, a pilgrim in this world? Then look again at this picture. By his power, because of his great compassion, Jesus "transforms the desert into a place of rest and refreshment and life through the power of God."[1] The hungry, Luke says, "all ate and were satisfied," so that far more was left over than they had at first. Yes, Jesus calls us out of the world and into the desert with him. But there he feeds us himself. He satisfies our needs, even as the psalmist said, "Delight yourself in the LORD and he will give you the desires of your heart" (Ps. 37:4).

A Primer on Christian Ministry

There is one more thing we need to get out of this passage, the point that seems to have been most on Jesus' mind. First we have a sign of his deity, then the Exodus in microcosm. The third point this passage presents is a primer on Christian ministry.

It is clear that Jesus intended this episode as an opportunity to teach his disciples an important lesson. As he so often did, he put them on the spot, challenging them to respond to the situation. John's Gospel tells us, "He already had in mind what he was going to do" (6:6). All along he was teaching them about Christian ministry. In this miracle we have a four-point program that is every bit as important for our instruction as it was for the original Twelve.

The first thing we see is the motive Jesus presents for Christian ministry. There is a great contrast between Jesus' motivation and that of the disciples. All through this account Jesus was guided by his great compassion. He saw the people scattered as sheep, so he shepherded them; he found them unknowing, and so he taught them; he found them sick, and so he healed them; he found them hungry, and so he fed them. In striking contrast is the attitude of the disciples, who callously urged Jesus to send them away.

That is a challenge to every Christian. How easy it is to lift our faces out toward the masses of spiritually hungry people around us, to turn away and say, "Lord, send them somewhere else. There must be somewhere else for them to go, so don't bother us with them." But to us, our Lord Jesus says exactly what he said to the Twelve: "You feed them." Charles Haddon Spurgeon, preaching from this text, reflected some hundred years ago:

Behold before you, disciples of Christ, this very day, thousands of men, and women, and children, who are hungering for the bread of life. They hunger till they faint. They spend their money for that which is not bread, and their labour for that which satisfieth not. They fall down famished in your highways, perishing for lack of knowledge. . . . See ye, disciples of Christ, see ye the great need which is before your eyes. . . . Let the vision rise perpetually before your eyes. See your work. Great as it is, dispirited as you may be by the great multitude who crave your help, yet recognize the appeal to your faith. Let the magnitude of the mission drive you the more earnestly to the work instead of deterring you from it.[2]

The disciples were like us. Focused on themselves, they were indifferent to the plight of others. Faced with so great a problem, they turned away rather than doing what they could. To both them and us, Jesus Christ speaks out of his great compassion. He says, "You give them something to eat." His compassion is the motive that drives all true Christian ministry.

Next we see the manner of provision for Christ's ministry in this world. It is noteworthy that this miracle took place around Bethsaida, which was the hometown of several of the disciples—Philip, Andrew, and Simon Peter. They therefore knew something about the resources nearby and immediately despaired of coming up with food for so great a throng. Even if provisions were available, they would be far beyond the means of this little band. John's Gospel tells that Philip responded to Jesus, "Eight months' wages would not buy enough bread for each one to have a bite!" (6:7). Because of the magnitude of the problem they despaired of a solution, considering it not merely difficult but impossible.

Here is where Andrew brought the little boy who holds such a special place in the record of Scripture. John 6:8–9 tells of his brief and wonderful appearance: "Another of his disciples, Andrew, Simon Peter's brother, spoke up, 'Here is a boy with five small barley loaves and two small fish, but how far will they go among so many?'" The boy did not have much, but he did the right thing, which is to offer it to Jesus. "How far can this go?" the disciple asked. Jesus thought it could go quite far, so he gathered the people for the feast he would provide.

Here is a great principle for provision in Christian ministry and our second point: you take what you have and bring it to Jesus Christ. Are our resources far too small to feed the hungry world with the gospel of Christ, or even the city in which God has placed us? Certainly they are, but that is no reason for us to despair, to turn away, to withhold whatever it is that we do have. Instead we must bring what we have to Jesus Christ, asking him to give the blessing and to meet our need.

That raises the question How much of what you have should you bring to the Lord? The answer is, Everything you have, which is not much. All that you are and all that you have—your money, your time, your talents, your experiences—consecrate all your meager provision to the Lord, and he will distribute them in abundance to the hungry. The best investment you can ever make is what this little boy did: offer what you have to Jesus, and he will spread blessing to many.

Then we read that Jesus took the loaves and fish and "looking up to heaven, he gave thanks and broke them" (Luke 9:16). Again, there is a contrast. Where had the disciples been looking, where had they cast their eyes? They looked to their pockets, to the nearby town, to their own resources, seeking power to meet the problem there. That is why they were discouraged. In great contrast we read that Jesus lifted his own eyes to heaven. Here is the point—in Christian ministry we are to rely upon God's power and not our own. " 'Not by might, not by power, but by my Spirit,' says the LORD Almighty" (Zech. 4:6).

This is our the third point: we must look to heaven for our increase. As Paul said of his ministry: "I planted the seed, Apollos watered it, but God made it grow" (1 Cor. 3:6). This is why all of those who accomplished much for God have been strong in prayer. They realized their weakness, they realized the poverty of their means, but they looked to God's power for blessing. They spoke the words of Psalm 20:7, "Some trust in chariots and some in horses, but we trust in the name of the LORD our God." They stood before the world as Moses with his back to the Red Sea, saying, "Do not be afraid. Stand firm and you will see the deliverance the LORD will bring you today. . . . The LORD will fight for you; you need only to be still" (Ex. 14:13–14).

Finally, we must do what Jesus had the disciples do, namely, to act in faith. Luke 9:16 says, "Taking the five loaves and the two fish and looking up to heaven, he gave thanks and broke them. Then he gave them to the disciples to set before the people." That too is what we must do. Looking out upon the hungry world with the compassionate eyes of Jesus, presenting to him all of the little we have, turning our hearts to God to bless and empower the work, we then must act in faith, believing that God will do his work in his way with the same power that fed the five thousand from the hands of Jesus Christ. How often those who would do great things for Christ began with no idea of the scale of their success but acted in faith because they believed in the power of God to bless his work!

Let's apply this briefly, and for a change of pace I will begin with myself. First, what is the motive for a true gospel minister? Is it desire for praise and honor? Is it the joy of long hours pondering Scripture and learned books? Is it the longing to tell people what you think about everything? The only true motive for a preacher of the gospel is the one set forth by this text—the compassion of Jesus Christ for a hungry world.

What then is the provision of the Christian minister? Surely a preacher must study and read; he must think and write things out. But all of that amounts to nothing unless the labor is consecrated to Jesus Christ, that is, placed into his hands. This means that the first concern of a preacher is never clever thoughts or brilliant construction or sophisticated expressions. Yes, a preacher must be a diligent workman, offering his best to the Lord. But his first concern must be faithfulness to Jesus, to whom his preaching first is presented. By the way, that also means that a true ministry need not rely on manipulative devices, does not descend to cheap marketing, does not pander to the audience but feeds the hungry with bread that Jesus gives, namely, his Word.

Where then does the power for true preaching come from? To where should the preacher look? To personality and dynamism? To his foolproof homiletical formula? No, the power for true preaching, for really moving the wills of people, comes only from God. A preacher must therefore look to heaven for blessing, and that will mean fervent and frequent prayer.

Finally, a gospel minister must act in faith, preaching not with self-confidence but with holy boldness. If I expect results I must preach by faith, not with timidity or fear but with the confidence that comes from faith in God to bless his Word, genuinely expecting him to convert the lost and edify the saints by the foolishness of preaching.

Now let me apply this to you. What must be your motive as you minister to those around you at work, in your families, in your neighborhoods? Should it not be the love of God that is in Christ? Should you not be burdened by compassion, by a desire for the spiritual benefit of those around you? But you have so little. Your words are so awkward, your arguments fall in the air. You do not have the buttons to push, the levers to pull to open the eyes of the blind at work, to lead your children in right paths, to persuade those bound by chains of darkness. Therefore take what you have, what you can do, and put it all in Jesus' hands. Then pray to God, looking to him for blessing, returning refreshed and bold in your labor because you trust in him. That is the way of Christian ministry, the primer that our Lord Jesus set before the Twelve in the feeding of this great multitude.

An Invitation to Come

Finally, this passage gives a wonderful invitation to any who stand outside the circle of Christ's provision. You are not a part of this Exodus throng; you have yet to turn their back on Egypt with its pleasures and bondage to sin. You labor for food that does not satisfy. You long for drink that does not well up to eternal life. Does this great miracle not show all that is in Jesus? Is it not obvious that this is a perishing world, a wilderness road that leads either to destruction or to life? To everyone today, the same Jesus who fed the multitude cries out still: "'I am the bread of life. He who comes to me will never go hungry, and he who believes in me will never be thirsty. . . . Whoever eats my flesh and drinks my blood has eternal life, and I will raise him up at the last day'" (John 6:35, 54).

Why then will you go hungry? Why should you perish? Come to him, believe on him, cover your sins with the blood of the Lamb, and you will be saved. He will feed you and lead you into eternal life.

Miracles and the Cross

Luke 9:37–45

while everyone was marveling at all that Jesus did,
he said to his disciples, "Listen carefully to what I am about
to tell you: The Son of Man is going to be betrayed
into the hands of men." (LUKE 9:43–44)

One of the things that attracted me to a study of the miracles is that they focus us on Jesus and his work for our salvation. I can hardly think of anything more important for us than this—to take our eyes off the world, off ourselves, off our works, and even off our faith, so that we may place them onto Jesus Christ. In the miracles we find that Jesus does the work needed to deliver us from weakness and condemnation, from danger and sickness, from death and from

the grip of the devil. We do not have power to save ourselves, much less other people, but the miracles point us to
our only hope, the One who is mighty to save.

Another thing the miracles do is instruct us on how
Christianity works—that is, the pattern and dynamics of
salvation as presented in the Scriptures. They bring alive
for us a biblical portrait of our own condition. We are the
ones pictured by lepers and paralytics, the sick and the dead
and the demon-possessed. In the miracles we also observe
Jesus in action. They show us his compassion, his willingness to heal and to touch and to save—and most of all his
ability to do so. Jesus, we find, is willing and able, for he is
the God of our salvation.

A Wide Perspective on Jesus' Ministry

This passage from Luke 9 is helpful in this regard, because it presents a progression for viewing Christ's saving
work. This miracle occurs upon Jesus' descent from the
Mount of Transfiguration. After Peter's great confession,
the climax of the Galilean phase of Jesus' ministry, our Lord
took his three closest disciples up on the mount and there
was revealed in all his heavenly glory. With him were
Moses and Elijah "in glorious splendor, talking with Jesus"
(Luke 9:31). Their topic was the cross, the destination that
was before Jesus. Peter and James and John worshiped in
awe, and they heard the voice from heaven as it declared,
"This is my Son, whom I have chosen; listen to him"
(9:35).

Our passage begins at Luke 9:37, when in the morning
Jesus and the three came down from the mountain back
into the valley, back down into the world, as it were. It
seems that there is an obvious parallelism at work between

Jesus' descent from the mountain, where he stood in his glory, down into the valley, and his descent from heaven into the world in the incarnation. Where, after all, are Moses and Elijah in the time after their death but in heaven? For Jesus to be in their midst reveals his heavenly glory and authority. Then, just as he came down from heaven to the manger, Jesus now comes down from the mountain back into the world.

That symbolism presents some valuable lessons for us. For one thing, we see that the work Jesus came into the world to do was his death upon the cross. That is what he was talking about with Moses and Elijah—the mission he was embarking upon (Luke 9:31). It is no surprise that after Jesus casts out the demon down in the valley he speaks again of the cross to his disciples. Jesus came into this world not just to give a moral example, not to establish a kingdom of worldly power and glory and affluence, but to die for our sins at the hands of men and then call us to join him in that cross. That is the task or work for which he came into the world.

In this passage Jesus came down from the mountain to encounter two forces that must be overcome. We are going to examine both of these: first, the devil and his spiritual powers, and second, the unbelief of Jesus' own disciples.

Finally, this miracle account, with its wide perspective on Jesus' saving ministry, reveals that the task Jesus came to perform, dying on the cross, is also the source of his victory over all that opposes him. Perhaps the main purpose of this passage is to show us the two choices open to Jesus and his use of great power. There is the way of glory and the way of the cross. Jesus might well have employed his awesome power for worldly glory and might. That is what Satan had tempted him to do in the desert, to take what had been

promised him without the inconvenience of the cross. Instead he followed the path of obedience to the Father, a
path that led him away from glory and to the cross. It is
from that cross that his power for salvation flows into this
world; it is by the cross that his kingdom advances even today. That is the theme of this chapter, the point he was
making to his disciples in Luke 9:23: "If anyone would
come after me, he must deny himself and take up his cross
daily and follow me."

Jesus versus the Devil

Luke is one of the Synoptic Gospels, along with
Matthew and Mark, so called because of the striking simi-
larities among them. Nonetheless the various writers have
distinctive interests and emphases, just as we would expect.
In the case of this miracle, Mark and Matthew emphasize
the importance of faith, but Luke has a different emphasis.
Luke omits a great deal of material that is found in Mark's
Gospel, material that must have been available to him. He
presented this miracle in nine verses compared with Mark's
nineteen. The argument with the scribes, Jesus' conversation with the boy's father, and the explanation for the disciples' failure are all missing here. The reason, it seems, that
Luke compressed his account was to bring this miracle into
the closest relationship with the passage that precedes it,
the transfiguration of Jesus on the mountain. I. Howard
Marshall explains what Luke is up to:

> It is the Jesus who has been transfigured who now
> appears to help men at the foot of the mountain;
> what the disciples cannot do, he can do. . . . The
> lesson of the transfiguration—that the gloriously re-

vealed Son of God must suffer—is reinforced: the Son of man who has power to heal must be betrayed by the unbelieving people whom he would gladly help.[1]

Jesus came down from heaven, down from the mount, to face two great battles. The first of these appears as this father cries out to Jesus. Luke tells us, "A man in the crowd called out, 'Teacher, I beg you to look at my son, for he is my only child. A spirit seizes him and he suddenly screams; it throws him into convulsions so that he foams at the mouth. It scarcely ever leaves him and is destroying him'" (9:38–39).

Jesus' ministry in the world requires him to battle the devil. This is a pattern that was established earlier at Jesus' baptism. Then, as in the transfiguration, the voice from heaven pronounced him God's Son. Immediately after, Jesus went out into the desert to be tempted by the devil. Given that example and the one in this passage, it is clear that Jesus came to earth to overthrow the devil and his work.

This is the third demon possession we have encountered in these studies of Jesus' miracles. In an earlier chapter we explored the subject in detail, so I will not do that now. But there are three points to notice from this encounter between Jesus and the demon, beginning with this: the devil's work is to enslave and distort human beings. Humanity was made in God's image, but the devil would twist us into his own. That is what he did in the garden when he tempted our first parents, and that is what the demons are found doing all through the Gospels.

The symptoms presented in this case resemble epilepsy. The boy convulses and foams at the mouth, falling to the ground. But there is far more than that. Mark's account tells us that he was also deaf and mute. He adds that the demon "has often thrown him into fire or water to kill him" (Mark 9:22). This is an excellent picture of what the devil is doing to people in this world. We are not up against a silly man in a red costume casting little darts our way. The devil's powers work within us, within our hearts and minds, leading us to self-destruction. They scar and destroy men and women made to bear God's image in the world.

Do not think you are lucky to avoid such a fate because you do not show the symptoms this boy does. Many, even most, people are firmly in the grip of a possession that is if anything stronger than this. Their minds have been captured by the demonic forces of materialism, sensual perversity, self-indulgent promiscuity, self-absorbed ambition. If that describes you, then God's image is being just as efficiently warped in your case as it was in this boy's. Your destruction is all the more horrible for the ease with which it is accomplished and the economy of effort it affords the devil.

Second, we need to notice that the combat described in this passage is between Jesus and the devil. We are not direct participants in this fight; rather, we are its object. We do not lend military aid to Jesus, nor does he need it.

The situation between Jesus and the devil is well illustrated by the battle between David and Goliath in the Old Testament (1 Sam. 17). Goliath was the horrifying giant who threatened and humiliated the hosts of Israel. What Israel needed, what we need before so great a foe, is a Savior. Jesus, like David, is just that. It is Christ's work to destroy the devil; ours is to stand firm and, as the Bible teaches, "see the deliverance the LORD will bring" (Ex. 14:13). He is the Victor; we are the beneficiaries of his triumph.

Third, we see in this passage Christ's absolute power to conquer the devil. In the presence of Jesus, the demon threw all his reserves into the fray. "Even while the boy was coming, the demon threw him to the ground in a convulsion," Luke writes (9:42). "But Jesus rebuked the evil spirit, healed the boy and gave him back to his father." The emphasis is on the ease with which Jesus succeeds in battle. The demon's power over the boy is unchallenged, but so also is Christ's over the demon. With just his word of rebuke, the devil's servant is chased from the field.

From all this we should draw three important lessons. First, do not toy with the devil or with sin; their purpose is to destroy you. Second, do not mistake yourself for the Savior but rather stand in faith, relying on his mighty victory. Third, because this mighty God is for us, we should not be afraid. Martin Luther said it best in his great hymn, "A Mighty Fortress Is Our God":

> And though this world, with devils filled
> should threaten to undo us,
> We will not fear, for God hath willed
> his truth to triumph through us.
> The prince of darkness grim,
> we tremble not for him;
> His rage we can endure,
> for lo! his doom is sure;
> One little word shall fell him.

Christ's Lament over Unbelief

The devil, however, is only one of the forces opposed to Jesus' work. The second opponent for him to overcome is the unbelief of his own disciples, and it was, if not stronger, more distressing to our Lord. This unbelief is highlighted when Jesus learns that the nine disciples he had left in the valley were unable to cast out this demon from the boy. " 'O unbelieving and perverse generation,' Jesus replied, 'how long shall I stay with you and put up with you?'" (Luke 9:41).

We need to be clear that it was the disciples to whom Jesus was speaking. This is less clear in the other Gospel accounts, but it is evident in Luke. The nine disciples had failed, and the reason was their unbelief. Jesus had been gone from them for only a little time, perhaps just a night, and they had fallen apart. We are reminded of Moses' similar departure to the mountaintop, leaving his followers alone. When Moses returned, Aaron and the Israelites were dancing around the golden calf. Perhaps it is fortunate Jesus was only gone as long as he was! He associates their failure to cast out the demon—a task they had been charged with and empowered to do by faith (see Luke 9:1, 6)—with the unbelief of Israel. If this situation was lesser in magnitude to what Moses discovered below Mount Sinai, it was cut from the same cloth. Therefore Jesus, having rebuked the devil, now rebukes his other great foe, the unbelief of his disciples.

"O unbelieving and perverse generation," Jesus laments. He does not mean by this that the disciples had no faith but that it was so enfeebled by their unbelief that it was unable to bear fruit. Compared with the mass of their unbelief, what faith they had was imperceptible. The term *perverse* indicates a twisted and distorted state that is the result of unbelief. These two always go together—an unbelieving generation will as a matter of course become a twisted one.

How are we to view this singular outburst by our Lord? Is this an unholy frustration, of the kind you and I experience? Is this sinful anger bursting forth with venom?

There is frustration and anguish in Jesus' words, but not sinfully or maliciously so. They are words like those spoken by a schoolteacher faced with students who won't do their homework. "O perverse generation! How long must I put up with you?" she says, when she intends to give at least a year of her life to their patient instruction. A pastor feels this way with his congregation that never absorbs what is preached. "O unbelieving generation! How long shall I stay with you?" he laments, knowing that he will give the whole of his life to their spiritual care. This is what parents say to their wayward children, an impatience for growth that flows out of boundless love. This is the kind of thing wives say to husbands who seem constitutionally unable to come home from work in time for dinner. "O perverse husband!" she cries. "How long will I put up with you?" Yet she has every intention of putting up with him for the rest of her life.

The great Scottish preacher Alexander Maclaren describes Jesus' lament as "a little window into a great matter." It is a little window because it shows only briefly a small portion of the great burden Jesus bore in his humanity. Jesus offered so great a treasure, invested so colossal an effort, poured out such love and sacrifice for the disciples, only to encounter persistent unbelief in their hearts. Maclaren writes:

> Because of their unbelief He knew that they could not receive what He desired to give them. . . . He has to turn from them, bearing it away unbestowed, like some man who goes out in the morning with his seed-basket full, and finds the whole field where he would fain have sown covered already with springing weeds or encumbered with hard rock, and has to bring back the germs of possible life to bless

and fertilize some other soil. . . . It is wonderfully pathetic and beautiful, I think, to see how Jesus Christ knew the pains of wounded love that cannot get expressed because there is no heart to receive it.[2]

Do not think that Jesus bears any less sorrow now that he is ascended into heaven, for it is in his humanity that he ministers there. He is in heaven now as God and man, with the same tender heart so wounded by the disciples' unbelief. How often he must look on us who are no different from these nine, upon a generation in the church that is no better and may be quite a lot worse than this fledgling group. He has given us faith so that we are his, and yet we are so unwilling to employ it. How many times has Jesus looked for faith in you and me, faith he has labored for and earned, faith he would use to reveal himself to many and bring true blessing to our lives, and yet has found an unbelief that will not receive him? Surely he cries out now, "O unbelieving and perverse generation! How long shall I stay with you and put up with you?"

Undoubtedly this opposing force, the unbelief of his own disciples, scored wounds against Jesus far deeper than any demon could ever inflict. Jesus overcame the demon by a rebuke. Will he overcome this foe, and if so, how? The answer is, I think, found within his lament. "How long shall I endure you?" Jesus cried. He said that in response to their weakness of faith, their immaturity, their worldly attitudes—and it is by enduring that he will overcome them. "How long?" he laments. The rest of Luke's Gospel gives the answer: as long as it takes. Jesus overcomes our unbelief by his patient care and long-suffering grace.

Jesus did not cast the disciples aside, and he will not cast you out either, if you have genuine faith, however small or weak. These disciples had shown they could not be trusted alone, so Jesus does not yet leave them. Their root was not yet established, so he would continue to tend and water them. How ready Jesus must have been to climb back up to the mountain of heaven, to ascend back to his place of glory. Yet he stayed among his needy little flock; he took them with him; he taught and protected them.

That was true in his days on earth, and Jesus' present ministry is no different in character. How will Jesus overcome the problem of your unbelief? By that same long-suffering love. Paul writes, "He who began a good work in you will carry it on to completion" (Phil. 1:6). Jesus will preserve all who trust in him, and he will bear with us until we are safely home.

HIGH PRIEST

The Way of the Cross

The passage concludes with Jesus turning to his disciples while the crowd marveled at the miracle he had performed. Luke 9:43–44 tells us, "While everyone was marveling at all that Jesus did, he said to his disciples, 'Listen carefully to what I am about to tell you: The Son of Man is going to be betrayed into the hands of men.'" This is obviously the climax to the whole account, and a matter of great importance. Whenever Jesus says, "Listen carefully," we need to do that or we will miss something essential.

What the disciples were to know, and what they still failed to grasp, was that Jesus would not ascend an earthly throne to rule but would instead ascend a cross to die. Luke tells us they could not absorb or assimilate this. It was hidden from them, we read, apparently because the time was not yet right. From the human perspective the next passage shows us why (Luke 9:46–48), for there the disciples are

seen arguing over their own relative supremacy. Seeking
their own victory and glory, it is no wonder they could not
accept the cross.

There is a contrast here that makes this point abun-
dantly clear—a contrast between the applause of the world
and the cross of Christ. This is, if anything, the key point
of this passage. It is to highlight this contrast that Luke has
compressed this miracle account toward the transfiguration. Jesus came down into the world, where he was confronted by the devil and by unbelief. By which route will he
conquer? Will it be the way of worldly glory and power—
the way the crowd desires him to go—or the way of death
and weakness and humiliation? Jesus makes it plain that his
way and the way for all who follow him is not the way of
glory but the way of the cross.

All of Jesus' victories were achieved by way of the cross.
It was there that he defeated and disarmed the devil. He did
so by paying the penalty for our sin, so that Satan can no
longer accuse us or torment us with fear. Jesus' death un-
dermined the whole of Satan's empire, because his atoning
work sets us free and reconciles us to God.

It is also by way of the cross that Jesus overcomes our
unbelief. It is sometimes said that the cross wins our hearts
by the fine example of love that it sets. That is not true.
Certainly Christ's great sacrifice *ought* to win the love of all
the world, but it does not and has not because of our
wickedness. It is not by moral influence that Jesus overcomes unbelief but by the Holy Spirit he earned the right
to send. Because of the Spirit's work Christ's elect are born
again, so that with enlivened hearts we receive what otherwise we loathed and despised. All through our lives that en-
livening work goes on, our unbelief more and more driven
out and replaced by willing faith.

The cross alone is Christ's banner in this world, quite in contrast to the way of glory. This difference was important to Martin Luther, who spoke of theologians of glory versus theologians of the cross. One way to tell the difference, he said, is through their opinion of suffering. To theologians of glory, suffering is a mistake, a problem, something to be explained and escaped. They expect to know and serve God apart from the suffering.

Not so the theologian of the cross. He regards suffering as the way to the knowledge of God. Not because suffering has any existential value in itself. No, the point is that in suffering we despair of all earthly power and glory and hope, looking for and finding the God who is hidden in sorrow. Luther wrote of suffering that "in so far as it takes everything away from us, [it] leaves us nothing but God: it cannot take God away from us, and actually brings Him closer to us."[3] That is what Paul was getting at in Philippians 3:10–11: "I want to know Christ and the power of his resurrection and the fellowship of sharing in his sufferings, becoming like him in his death, and so, somehow, to attain to the resurrection from the dead."

How little of this we find today, and its absence explains the weakness of the church. This, for instance, is what is wrong with today's seeker-sensitive movement. Despite good intentions to reach the unchurched, this movement has pursued not the cross but the way of glory. We are told to focus on pleasing the target audience, to seek their applause and approval, to cater to the tastes of the crowd. We have forgotten what Jesus did, turning away from the consumer audience to face the cross.

You cannot accuse Jesus of lacking compassion, and yet he turned away from the consumers and the praise of men. Christ was given over into the hands of men and put to death. Today's theologians of glory are giving over the church into those same hands, and they will put it to death as once they did him.

Disturbing News

In 1988 a tumor appeared in Dave Dravecky's left arm. He was a major-league baseball player, a left-handed pitcher. When a majority of his deltoid muscle was removed the doctor told him, "Outside of a miracle you will never pitch again." Being a Christian, Dravecky began praying for just that, and in August of the next year he was scheduled to pitch his comeback game. "I don't care what anybody says to me," he recalls. "It was a miracle."

We can imagine what went through his mind before that game: dreams of triumph, the camera then drawing close. He smiles and says, "First, I want to give all the glory to my Lord and Savior Jesus Christ." That is how we plan things—the way of glory, giving praise to Jesus out of our earthly victory. It is not a bad thing to praise Christ should we achieve great things; but we should not think that this is the way to know or serve Jesus in the world. It is through the cross that Christ's power shines into this world, because his is a resurrection power and comes only by death and the cross.

Things did not turn out the way Dravecky had hoped. In the sixth inning of that comeback game, his arm shattered as he threw a fastball. He lay in agony on the grass, and as they wheeled him off, he remembered the words a Christian friend had told him that afternoon that the miracles of God come by the cross and not by baseball glory.

During long treatments, multiple surgeries, and ultimately the amputation of his arm, Dravecky and his wife battled depression, fear, and pain. He found it quite a bit harder to praise God from the valley of his hospital bed than from the mount of glory that is the pitcher's mound. But he did learn to praise God there, for in tribulation he sought God and learned of his great goodness. He writes, "What God does through the valleys of life is He shapes and molds us into the image that He wants us to be. He gives us strength to endure."[4] That is something he learned not on the mount but in the valley, not by way of glory but by way of the cross.

Dravecky never got to tell the world how happy God made him by making him a superstar and a millionaire and a comeback miracle. But out of his trials, his testimony impacted thousands of people who heard him praise a God who sustained him in loss.

It will be the same for you if you are a Christian. It is not by the way you rise to the top of the corporate ladder that you will reveal the glory of Christ to this world, but by the way you trust him with joy when you are downsized out of your position, when rivals attack you, when people have turned against you and your security is threatened. You do not have to become rich, have perfect smiling children, or become famous in this world to serve the kingdom of Christ. He calls his own to the cross, rich and poor, and there we find and follow him.

That was the message of the transfiguration, that Christ's glory is revealed by way of the cross. In the same way, it will not be the glare of camera lights that produces our own transfiguration, our own opportunity to reflect the glory of Christ out into the world. It is the light of the open tomb, the resurrection power of the new creation, shining through the cross. By faith in sorrow, by joy in darkness, by calmness of spirit and forgiving love in the midst of tribulation, it is by the cross that we reveal to others a kingdom and a Christ that are not of this world.

Does this news dismay you, the way it did the disciples? Jesus said, "I tell you the truth, unless a kernel of wheat falls to the ground and dies, it remains only a single seed. But if it dies, it produces many seeds" (John 12:24). If you have success and glory, yes, go ahead and give credit to God. But understand that heartache and pain will come to you; they are always with us. In them, and not in our glory, is where our transfiguration takes place. "May I never boast," Paul declared, "except in the cross of my Lord Jesus Christ" (Gal. 6:14). For there alone the salvation of God is revealed to us and through us to the world.

Opposition to the Miracles

Luke 11:14–26

*Now if I drive out demons by Beelzebub, by whom do your
followers drive them out? So then, they will be your judges.
But if I drive out demons by the finger of God, then the
kingdom of God has come to you.* (LUKE 11:19–20)

Chapter 9 is the turning point of Luke's Gospel. There Peter makes his great confession, Jesus is transfigured on the
mount, and Christ's death on the cross is asserted as the
central principle of his ministry. The chapters before that
contain a great many miracles, but the next ten, chapters
10 through 19, have very few. The reason for this is a shift
in Jesus' strategy. The miracles served to reveal him as the
Messiah. But once Peter and the other disciples had ac-

knowledged Jesus as such, he focused mainly on their instruction, as well as on the mounting opposition of those who would eventually conspire to put him to death.

It is that opposition that this passage from Luke 11 focuses on. We begin with yet another miracle in which Jesus casts out an evil spirit. Having presented this kind of thing several times already, Luke does not dwell on the details but rather draws our attention to the response from those who were watching. Naturally many people marveled at what they saw; we see that in verse 14, although that does not mean that they understood or believed on Jesus as the Savior. Verse 16 says that others who were there tested Jesus by asking for a sign from heaven, as if what he had just done was not enough of a sign. That is the way unbelief works—it never has enough evidence.

But the worst manifestation of unbelief appears in Luke 11:15, and it is with this that our passage principally deals: "Some of them said, 'By Beelzebub, the prince of demons, he is driving out demons.'" In the Greek text the name is Beelzebul, meaning "lord of the house," and obviously a reference to Satan. The reason Jesus can drive out demons, they said, is that he is in league with the devil.

Luke does not identify the authors of that terrible accusation. Mark says it was "teachers of the law who came down from Jerusalem" (3:22). Matthew is even more specific, identifying them as "the Pharisees" (12:24). The picture is clear: these were representatives of the religious establishment who came to check out what was going on with this Jesus of Nazareth. They saw what he did and did not in any way dispute that a true miracle had taken place. The key question had to do with its source. If it was a true miracle, the author must be either God or the devil, and these Pharisees asserted that it was the latter.

Jesus' Fivefold Reply

The majority of this passage consists of Jesus' severe rebuke to this false indictment. Mark says that Jesus spoke to them in parables (3:25), by which he means not the long stories we think of but blunt, pithy sayings that served to dismantle the accusation and confront the accusers. There are five points to Jesus' reply, and I want to work briefly through each of them. When that is done, we will focus specifically on what Jesus said about two vital topics—his own saving work and the unbelief of those who oppose him.

The first thing Jesus does is overthrow the rational basis of the accusation. He shows that the objection is not based on logical deduction but rather sheer animosity toward him: "Any kingdom divided against itself will be ruined, and a house divided against itself will fall. If Satan is divided against himself, how can his kingdom stand? I say this because you claim that I drive out demons by Beelzebub" (Luke 11:17–18).

His point is to expose the illogic of the accusation. How could Jesus be manifesting Satan's power, when it is Satan who is suffering by his ministry? Is Satan at war within his own kingdom? If he is then he is no longer a concern; his collapse will soon occur and demon possession will cease to be a problem. People, I suppose, might argue that a ruse, a deception, might be at work so that Satan is promoting his champion by making him appear to be what he is not. Such a suggestion is ludicrous to those who had observed Jesus' ministry, as we have done through these studies of the miracles. The sheer ferocity of Jesus' assault on demonic strongholds, the desperation of their resistance, and the completeness of his victories mark this as real warfare and no mere ruse.

& whose demons are being cast out

To this, Jesus adds another remark that exposes the hypocrisy of the Pharisees' claim: "Now if I drive out demons by Beelzebul, by whom do your followers drive them out? So then, they will be your judges" (Luke 11:19). This seems to acknowledge that Jesus was not the only one casting out demons. We find corroboration of this in Mark 9:38, where the disciples tell of an unknown man who was casting out demons in Jesus' name; Jesus told them then not to interfere. Other ancient writings, such as the writings of Josephus and various rabbinic materials, also tell about exorcisms.[1]

Jesus' point, however, is to expose the hypocrisy of the Pharisees' logic. What they approve of in others they condemn in Jesus. Their reasoned arguments have fallen to the ground; their unreasoned animosity is exposed for all to see. This is why Jesus concludes, "They will be your judges," by which he means that their approval of Jewish exorcists condemns their disapproval of Jesus.

Jesus builds upon this in the second point of his argument: "Now if I drive out demons by the finger of God, then the kingdom of God has come to you" (Luke 11:20). The point is not merely that casting out demons—whether by Jesus or by the Jewish exorcists—represents an application of God's power. There is a sense in which that can well be said. But there is more. What Jesus is saying is that his coming and the manner of his overthrow of Satan specifically signifies God's saving reign upon the earth. The "I" here is emphatic. "If *I* drive out demons," he says, then God's kingdom has come to you.

What are we to make of this expression, "the finger of God"? Matthew renders it as "by the Spirit of God" (12:28), so obviously there is a connection with the Holy Spirit. Jesus casts out demons by the Holy Spirit, who is God's finger, his executor, in this world.

It seems that Jesus' point is to contrast his own manner of casting out demons with that of the Jewish exorcists he has just referred to. Just as there was a qualitative difference in the manner of his teaching compared with that of the Jewish leaders—Jesus was said to teach "with authority" (Luke 4:32)—there is also a qualitative difference between Jesus' war on the demons and that of the exorcists. They relied upon mechanical devices and external means. They burned incense, used various medicines, laid hands, employed water, played music. The ancient literature is filled with all sorts of devices, some mundane and some bizarre.[2] In striking contrast, Jesus cast out demons "by the finger of God," with authority and power, by means of a simple command.

There is more, however, to this expression than that. We have already seen in these studies that Luke sees a thematic parallel between Jesus' saving work and the Exodus, when Moses led the Israelites out from bondage in Egypt. Here, it seems, we have yet another connection, for the "finger of God" was the description Pharaoh's magicians gave of Moses' miracle-working power.

Moses was pitted against Pharaoh's sorcerers, magicians who wielded real power derived from the devil (that is, Beelzebul). In that conflict, Moses' power from God overthrew Pharaoh's magicians with terrible and violent effects to the realm of Satan. When these magicians were forced to admit their failure, they lamented to Pharaoh, "This is the finger of God" (Ex. 8:19).

Before Moses died, he foretold another like himself who would come. Deuteronomy 18:18–19, a famous and important passage, relays what God revealed to Moses: "I will raise up for them a prophet like you from among their brothers; I will put my words in his mouth, and he will tell them everything I command him. If anyone does not listen to my words that the prophet speaks in my name, I myself will call him to account."

In light of this, by wielding the very finger of God against the kingdom of Satan, Jesus asserts that they are obliged to acknowledge him as the Messiah, the One foretold by Moses. Failure to do this is culpable negligence that will be punished by God.

Luke 11:21 begins a more developed parable, which presents Jesus' third response to the Pharisees. There is, he says, a strong man, heavily armed, who guards his house so that his possessions are safe. Obviously the reference here is to the devil, the house is his kingdom (remember that Beelzebul means "lord of the house"), and the possessions are the souls of the people he controls. Jesus goes on to describe his own work against the devil: "But when someone stronger attacks and overpowers him, he takes away the armor in which the man trusted and divides up the spoils" (v. 22). The meaning of this is clear, and we will come back to it later in this study.

Fourth, Jesus, having overcome the logic of their accusation, having then pressed on them the right understanding of his miracles, now makes his own accusation against the Pharisees. "He who is not with me is against me, and he who does not gather with me, scatters" (Luke 11:23). This would have been heard by his specific accusers and by all in the crowd who marveled at Jesus but did not commit themselves to him. If they are not for him, they are against him, and by implication they are allied with the devil. While Jesus is seeking to gather, they are opposing him, working to scatter along with Satan.

Finally, fifth, Jesus makes a point about a necessity laid upon those who benefit from his warfare on the demons.

His intent is not to lead us in speculation about the demonic. Rather, he shows that those who benefit from his saving work but do not press forward with full commitment end up worse off than before they started. If the demons who are cast out return later and find that no one else has moved into their former residence, then they will return with greater power than before so that, as Jesus concludes, "the final condition of that man is worse than the first" (Luke 11:26).

Jesus the Strong Man

Those five points make up Jesus' stinging rebuttal, all of which deal with two main issues. On the one hand we have Jesus' depiction of his saving work, articulated in terms of his battle with the devil. On the other is his assessment of the unbelief of his opponents. We will deal with each of these in turn, beginning with what this tells about Christ's work as Savior.

At the heart of this discourse is the brief parable of the strong man bound in his own house. We have already seen what it says about Satan. Apart from the stronger deliverer, the devil's hold on his victims is secure. "His possessions are safe," Jesus says, and that is precisely what we find in this world. Until Jesus and the gospel are proclaimed, the one thing we can be sure of is Satan's unchallenged dominion.

But Jesus flatly asserts that he is stronger than the devil. That seems implausible to many people, for whom Jesus epitomizes weakness. One thinks of the Soviet tyrant Josef Stalin's comment when he was warned that the Pope was concerned about his ambitions. "And how many armored divisions has the Pope?" he cynically replied, discounting the power of faith just as many underrate the power of

Christ.[3] Jesus was born not in a palace but in a stable, to poor, unknown parents in an obscure village. In his career he did not seek worldly power—money, prestige, political position; he actively shunned them. How then is he stronger than the devil, who always seems to have worldly power on his side?

Luke 11:22 explains this, saying that the stronger man overpowers the lord of the house, and "he takes away the armor in which the man trusted." The Greek word rendered as "armor" comes from the word *nike*, or "victory." It means not just defensive armor but the whole armory of weapons for ensuring victory, which are taken away here by the stronger man.

How does Jesus, in all his manifest weakness, take away Satan's mighty arsenal? First, we have to understand what the devil's real weapons are. Yes, the devil oppresses us through the various levers of worldly power he controls by his influence in the hearts of sinful people. We see his hand in the media, in government, in advertising, in the schools. But Satan's real power, the power that holds his possessions safely, is not worldly power but spiritual weaponry, as Paul said, "spiritual forces of evil in the heavenly realms" (Eph. 6:12).

What are Satan's spiritual weapons? The Bible emphasizes two of them. First of all, Satan is called "the Deceiver" (see John 8:44; 2 Cor. 2:11; 11:14; Rev. 12:9). That is how he led our first parents into his web, by lying to them, deceiving and tempting them to disobey God. Jesus overcomes this weapon by revealing the truth. This is what Jesus explained to Pontius Pilate during his trial: "For this reason I was born, and for this I came into the world, to testify to the truth" (John 18:37). Jesus is "the Word," and the truth he reveals break's Satan's hold of darkness. This is what the prophet foretold of him:

The people walking in darkness
    have seen a great light;
on those living in the land of the shadow of death
    a light has dawned. (Isa. 9:2)

Truth may seem like something weak, until we realize that the Word of God, the teaching of truth, takes one of Satan's strongest weapons out of his hand. That is why Christians, to serve God and resist the devil, must be people of truth, people of the Word of God.

Another biblical description of Satan is "the Accuser." This is how the devil is pictured in Zechariah 3:1, where Israel's high priest is seen standing before the angel of the Lord, with "Satan standing at his right side to accuse him." Accusation is Satan's most potent weapon. He points out our sin, points out our condemnation under God's holy law, and thus lays hold of us for his own kingdom. He accuses us, exults in our condemnation, and as the ruler of the kingdom of darkness binds us safely within his damned household.

That would seem to pose a great problem, because Satan's accusations are founded upon truth. We are sinners. We have violated God's law. God is a just Judge and must condemn us. How can bonds like that be broken, when they are founded on God's own Word and holy character?

The answer is found in Jesus' saving work, when his weakness overcame Satan's strength. Satan's greatest achievement was to tempt one of Jesus' disciples, Judas Iscariot, and lead him as he betrayed our Lord. He orchestrated a mock trial and an unjust execution so that God's Son would be crucified in weakness. And thereby Jesus plucked the sword from Satan's hand and laid it upon his throat. The Puritan Jonathan Edwards therefore wrote:

Satan, that old serpent, used a great deal of subtlety to procure Christ's death; and doubtless, when he had accomplished it, he thought he had obtained a complete victory, being then ignorant of the contrivance of our redemption. But the wisdom of Christ so ordered things that Satan's subtlety and malice should be made the very means of undermining the foundations of his kingdom; and so He wisely led him into the pit that he had dug.[4]

Here is one of the great truths of the Christian faith, that Christ's weakness has overcome the devil's strength; his death has achieved life for us. Saint Augustine long ago observed just this, writing:

The devil was conquered precisely when he was thought to be conquering, namely, when Christ was crucified. For at that moment the blood of him who had no sin at all, was shed for the remission of our sins. The devil deservedly held those whom he had bound by sin to the condition of death. So it happened that One who was guilty of no sin freed them justly from this condemnation.[5]

By his death on the cross, Jesus took the weapons out of Satan's hands and broke the bonds that held sinners captive. Then, by rising from the dead, ascending into heaven, and sending his Holy Spirit into the world, Jesus secures his own triumph by bringing sinful men and women to saving faith. No more will Satan accuse us for our sin, for we have been redeemed. So great is this news that the Book of Revelation sets it forth as the very song of heaven: "Now have come the salvation and the power and the kingdom of our

God, and the authority of his Christ. For the accuser of our brothers, who accuses them before our God day and night, has been hurled down. They overcame him by the blood of the Lamb and by the word of their testimony" (Rev. 12:10–11).

Jesus' victory is the triumph of one kingdom over another on the spiritual field of battle. That is the second way these teachings relate to Christian salvation. Jesus emphasized this in Luke 11:20: "If I drive out demons by the finger of God, then the kingdom of God has come to you." His saving work represents the overthrow of one kingdom by another, the kingdom of Satan and darkness by the kingdom of God and of light.

What happens when one kingdom triumphs in battle, conquering or reconquering a land? Several things happen. There is a change of administration, a change of agenda. There are new goals, new ways of doing things, and most of all a new allegiance that is demanded. That is exactly what happens when Christ conquers our enemy and lays hold of our hearts. If you turn to Jesus by faith for the forgiveness of your sin, you enter into a new kingdom. You have new obligations, and a new allegiance is demanded of you.

The emphasis is on the radical nature of the Christian faith and life. If you are a Christian, you do not have the privilege of mixed loyalties, halfhearted affections, and a lukewarm response to the call of Christ. He now is your king and demands your allegiance. If you are not with Jesus, you are against him; if you are not gathering with him, you are scattering against him. That, in Luke 11:23, is what Jesus would not let his adversaries ignore.

Finally, and this is the third point regarding Christ's salvation, it is not enough to benefit from Jesus in a superficial way. You must commit to him, you must admit him into the

house vacated by the devil. His Holy Spirit must take up
residence, or things will end up worse for you than before.
J. C. Ryle comments:

> There is no safety except in thorough Christianity.
> . . . The house must not only be swept and white-
> washed; a new tenant must be introduced. . . . The
> outward life must not only be decorated with the
> formal trappings of religion; the power of vital reli-
> gion must be experienced in the inner man. The
> Devil must not only be cast out; the Holy Spirit
> must take his place. Christ must dwell in our hearts
> by faith.[6]

Jesus' Critique of Unbelief

That is the core Christian message, which Jesus force-
fully pressed upon those unbelieving ears. At the same time
he delivered a telling assessment of those who accused him.
Christians are sometimes intimidated by those who oppose
Jesus and the Bible, but Jesus unmasks their unbelief, showing first how unreasonable it is.

It is often assumed that disbelief in the Bible, particularly that of the scientific sort, occupies the intellectual
high ground. Christians are simpler folks who can dupe
themselves into a faith that is irrational by its very character. Jesus explodes that idea, confronting the Pharisees with
the illogic of their accusation. "A house divided cannot
stand," he said, and then showed the hypocrisy that motivated their objection. "If I drive out the demons by Beelzebub, by whom do your followers drive them out?"

Rejection of Jesus Christ is not based upon superior reasoning. There is a reason why Psalm 14 says, "The fool says

in his heart, 'There is no God.'" If you have ever listened to the arguments for atheism you will find that to be the case. Yes, there are difficulties with faith in Christ and in the Bible, but, as Alexander Maclaren quipped, "They are gnats beside the camels which unbelief has to swallow."[7] This is why most people have retreated from a vigorous denial of God to the supposedly safer regions of agnostic indecision.

Agnostics rest on the supposition that there is no way to know if there is a God. It can't be proved either way, they say. But, as in the case of Jesus' opponents, there is a basic hypocrisy at work here. Agnostics espouse, often loudly, a position they admit cannot be proved on the grounds that it is wrong to hold a position unless you can prove it. Why then, we ask, are they agnostics? Having failed to supply a logical defense of agnosticism, agnostics instead have assumed it because it is what they want to believe.

The problem is not ignorance. This is what Paul explains in Romans 1. Unbelievers are not in ignorance of God's existence but in rebellion against his rule. The created realm, Paul explains, manifestly declares the being and power of God. Romans 1:19 says, "What may be known about God is plain to them, because God has made it plain to them." Why then do they not believe? Paul explains that unbelievers "suppress the truth by their wickedness. . . . For although they knew God, they neither glorified him as God nor gave thanks to him, but their thinking became futile and their foolish hearts were darkened" (Rom. 1:18, 21).

People withhold faith in Christ not out of ignorance but because they do not want a Lord, because they do not want heaven intruding on their earth, because they want to enjoy the pleasures of sin for a season while numbing their minds to the reality beyond. People do not reject Chris-

tianity because it fails to meet the test of reason, any more than these Pharisees rejected Jesus on rational grounds.

There is, of course, a reasoning to unbelief, but it is a reasoning that is enslaved to a hardened heart, slavishly opposed to the Word of God. If you accept unbelievers' assumptions, then the logic does follow. If you start with the Pharisees' assumption that Jesus must not be from God because he disagreed with them, then it follows that his power must be of Satan and not of God. If you accept the modernist assumption that miracles are by definition impossible, then it must be right that the biblical accounts of miracles are superstitious fabrications. If you accept the postmodern assumption that tolerance is the supreme virtue, then the Jesus who says these harsh and condemning words must be recast as something quite different. Starting with the assumptions, the arguments make sense. But the assumptions are wrong. They are of men and not God. They are of the devil and not of Christ, who has spoken in his Word.

Jesus dismantled the arguments of his accusers, and in his response he characterized their unbelief in three ways. They are self-condemning, because by rejecting Jesus, unbelievers expose their love of sin and evil, their bondage to the realm of Satan. Their unbelief is also self-defeating, for this Savior who casts out demons is the only strong man capable of breaking Satan's hold, of rescuing them from guilt and death. To reject him is to reject the only salvation. Finally, such unbelief is self-destroying. The condition Jesus spoke of in the final verse was pointedly true of these Pharisees. They were worse off than before they met him, than before they knew anything of religion; they were deeper in the devil's grips than ever before because they shut out the light of the gospel they had seen, which alone casts out darkness. Now they were, in opposing him, enemies of the Savior, scatterers under the devil's employ because of their unbelief.

Tongues to Speak

It is important to recognize that there are people who have yet to decide about Jesus Christ and are looking for a way to know the truth. Let me observe that the way of these Pharisees is not the right way. Indeed, what a contrast they present to the man with whom this account began, a man who was demon-afflicted and mute but had his mouth opened by Jesus Christ. The Pharisees were quick to speak, out of the wickedness of their hearts, and so they were unable to profess the faith in Christ that saves a sinner. This man, being mute, had obviously listened, and so he came to Jesus in faith. The Pharisees pitted their unbelief against Jesus, who easily exposed them. Instead they should have taken their questions to Jesus, who holds the power to loosen tongues to speak his praise.

In *Mere Christianity*, C. S. Lewis posed a question much like the one before these Pharisees. He pointed out that there is a choice we must make when confronted with what the Bible says about Jesus Christ. We cannot praise him as a great moral teacher, the way many do, but as nothing more. Jesus plainly identified himself as God incarnate, the Savior of the world. Our passage in this chapter presents just one example of this kind of claim. What, then, is he? He is either a lunatic of vast proportions, believing he is the world's Savior, or he is a liar comparable to the devil of hell, compared with whom every other megalomaniac pales into insignificance. Or he is the Son of God who commands our faith and allegiance. Lewis concludes,

Either this man was, and is, the Son of God: or else a madman or something worse. You can shut Him up for a fool, you can spit at Him and kill Him as a demon; or you can fall at His feet and call Him Lord and God. But let us not come with any patronising nonsense about His being a great human teacher. He has not left that open to us. He did not intend to.[8]

Maybe you don't know how to answer. In that case, Jesus has told us what to do. He said it in this chapter, which deals with deciding what to make of him: "Ask and it will be given to you; seek and you will find; knock and the door will be opened to you" (Luke 11:9).

If you are unable to speak the words of faith in Jesus Christ, to confess with your mouth that Jesus is Lord, the Savior of your soul, then take your mute lips to him. *Ask* him to reveal himself, and he will give you what you ask. *Seek* his truth in the Bible, and you will find the very Word of God. *Knock* on the door, the way to faith and salvation, the door through which light shines into the darkness of this world. And it will be opened for you. Jesus will open your mind and your heart and your mouth, and like this crowd, many will be amazed at the salvation God has revealed through you.

12

One Who Gave Thanks

Luke 17:11–19

*thanksgiving
faith*

*Were not all ten cleansed? Where are the other nine?
Was no one found to return and give praise to
God except this foreigner? (LUKE 11:17–18)*

One of the good rules for interpreting the miracles of Jesus Christ is that we should allow each account to make its particular point, without trying to make it a comprehensive portrait of salvation. That rule also holds for the parables, and perhaps the greatest example of this principle comes from the parable of the prodigal son. That story beautifully presents God's mercy for sinners who repent, but if it is pressed to be a comprehensive model of salvation it lacks, among other things, Christ's atoning sacrifice. The parable makes a powerful point, but it was not intended by our Lord to be an all-encompassing model.

When it comes to the miracles, we want to let each account show its particular angle on the ministry of Jesus Christ, without insisting that they be comprehensive. It is together that the miracles make their cumulative effect, drawing together the whole realm of fallen humanity in these portraits of the blind and lame, the dumb and demon-possessed, the leprous and the dead. Each miracle shows us something important about ourselves and about Christ's redeeming work. Each encounters the great compassion of Jesus Christ and finds abundant power in him.

The Lepers' Cry for Mercy

With that being said, we come in this chapter to a miracle account that, if not comprehensive, gives us an extensive view of Christian salvation. I say this because not only does it depict sinners before they come to Jesus and during the decisive encounter that brings them salvation, but also it opens a large window on what comes after, on the intended effects of Christ's saving work in people's lives.

We have seen in a previous study how leprosy so well depicts the corrupting power and the condemning presence of sin. Leprosy, like sin, worked death within while isolating its victims from fellowship with other people. Worst of all, under the old covenant law it barred them from fellowship with God. No condition was more feared or loathed than leprosy. Lepers were the walking dead, horrid portraits of sin's effects in this world.

Our account begins with not one but ten lepers. Luke tells us they were at a distance from the road, when they saw Jesus and "called out in a loud voice, 'Jesus, Master,

MERCY

have pity on us'" (Luke 17:13). The first thing we should note is that here is a cry that is always certain of a gracious and saving response.

To understand this we must first note the One to whom that cry was addressed. "Jesus!" they cried, and Jesus is One who is filled with compassion. It is well said his compassion is like water, always ready to flow downward into low places. He is "close to the brokenhearted and saves those who are crushed in spirit" (Ps. 34:18).

This is something we have learned about Jesus over and over in Luke's Gospel. In chapter 4, he is beset by crowds of people with all kinds of sickness. We read, "Laying his hands on each one, he healed them" (v. 40). In chapter 5, he saw the solitary leper, who cried out, "Lord, if you are willing, you can make me clean." Jesus replied, "I am willing" (vv. 12–13), and he always is willing to answer the cry of the needy. When Jesus, in chapter 7, came upon the widow of Nain bringing out the dead body of her only son, "His heart went out to her and he said, 'Don't cry'" (v. 13). And then he brought that boy back to life. Again and again we find Jesus eager to help the lowly and burdened, those crushed by the world, by sin and the devil. Because of his great compassion, you too may cry out to Jesus and be certain that you will find one ready to heal and to save.

There is another reason why this cry is certain of success, and that is its content. "Have pity on us," they cried. It was a cry to Jesus on the basis of his mercy, which is another way of translating the word for "pity." Many people, however, came to Jesus with a very different cry, and they received a very different response. All through Luke's Gospel we see people, often religious leaders, who came to Jesus not asking for mercy but demanding that he prove himself. Instead of "Have pity on us," they cried, "Prove

MERCY / NOT MERIT
PROOF

that you really are who you say!" Jesus consistently refused
to gratify that demand, arguing that his death on the cross
and resurrection from the grave would be proof enough (see
Luke 11:29–30). Therefore, if you cry to Jesus, demanding
that he give you a sign of his worth and power, you will find
that he has little interest in giving you what you want.

There is another way to call out to Jesus, a way that also
fails to receive his saving response. It is the cry spoken
about in the next chapter of Luke's Gospel, the parable of
the Pharisee and the tax collector. A Pharisee went into
the temple to pray. Jesus tells us that he "stood up and
prayed about himself: 'God, I thank you that I am not like
other men—robbers, evildoers, adulterers—or even like
this tax collector. I fast twice a week and give a tenth of all
I get'" (Luke 18:11–12). Here is the cry of a man who presents his merits, his deserving, his righteousness, as the
ground of his request to the Lord.

Jesus summed up this parable by saying the Pharisee
who spoke of his works was not accepted by God. Pointing
instead to the tax collector, a man who knew his sin but
cried out to God for mercy, Jesus said, "I tell you that this
man, rather than the other, went home justified before
God. For everyone who exalts himself will be humbled, and
he who humbles himself will be exalted" (Luke 18:14).

These lepers had done nothing for Jesus, nor could they
have. They stood at a great distance, knowing well their
unworthiness. They were as far as possible from what is
good and wholesome and commendable. And yet when
they cried, "Jesus, have mercy," they found free and ready
grace. That is a wonderful example that salvation is by
grace alone, through faith alone—not by works and most
certainly not by doubt. A cry of humble faith is always certain of a gracious and saving reply from Jesus.

Martin Luther, in a sermon on this text, says this about the cry that receives Christ's favor: "It allows no merit, will not purchase the grace of God with works, like the doubters and hypocrites do, but brings with it pure unworthiness, clings to and depends wholly on the mere unmerited favor of God, for faith will not tolerate works and merit in its company."[1]

A Display of Saving Faith

The first thing we see here is this excellent cry, to which Jesus replied with these words: "Go, show yourselves to the priests." This brings our second point, a display of the faith that is the condition of salvation. It is a faith that must believe on Jesus, that must believe what he has said, despite the considerable evidence to the contrary.

A little background will help us see what Jesus demanded of these ten lepers. Leviticus 13 provides regulations for handling infectious skin diseases like leprosy. Verses 45 and 46 are the ones that spelled so great a doom upon the lepers, for they said, "The person with such an infectious disease must wear torn clothes, let his hair be unkempt, cover the lower part of his face and cry out, 'Unclean! Unclean!' As long as he has the infection he remains unclean. He must live alone; he must live outside the camp."

That same chapter, however, also contained the procedures for the restoration of a leper who had been cleansed. He had to present himself to the priests; presumably in Jesus' day that would be in the temple at Jerusalem. The priests were provided with a whole battery of tests whereby they would declare the person clean or unclean. The unclean ones would be sent away. Those declared clean, how-

ever, were able to return to the life of the nation, partici-
pating in its religious rites and thus receiving again the
benefits of God's covenant.

We see then what Jesus was demanding these ten lepers
to do. "Go, show yourselves to the priests." We can imagine how they might well have responded. Knowing the cri-
teria of the priests' approval—if there was one portion of
Scripture these lepers knew, it would have been this one—
they might have cast their eyes on their bodies with dismay.
The splotches were still there! The last thing they wanted
to be told was to go show themselves to the priests. As they
were, this was an invitation for refusal, rejection, humiliation. I think we would understand if they had done a test
run, performing a trial inspection on one another, then ex-
claiming, "If we go to the priests, as Jesus says, we will be
condemned!"

Therefore how wonderful it is to read what they did.
Luke 17:14 says, "They went."

Here we have a penetrating display of what saving faith
requires. First it requires a faith in the authority of Jesus
Christ and in his Word. If anybody else had told these lepers, still foul, still rotting, still showing such corruption, we
would rightly reprove them for their folly. Such a person
would be making sport of them, mocking them, driving
home the hopelessness of their case. But what makes this
command so different is the One who gave it.

These lepers obviously had heard about Jesus' saving
power, which is why they thought to cry out to him. They
heard that this Jesus had driven out evil spirits. They
learned, perhaps as they eavesdropped on society, of how he
cured so many sick people and so many kinds of malady.
What they heard was good news of salvation—and they believed that good news. This is why they accepted Jesus' au-

thority when he told them to go to the priests. They knew that One who could do such works must bear divine power; therefore his word must also be divine, with authority over life and death and even leprosy.

These lepers remind us that we never waste our time or effort when we speak about the good things Jesus Christ has done, about his power for salvation, about his authority as the very Son of God. For from hearing comes faith, and from faith comes salvation (Rom. 10:14–15).

Faith is accepting the authority of the Word of Christ and acting on that belief. There is something else here about saving faith, however. It is vital for us to see that these lepers believed despite the contrary evidence of their senses. While their bodies still bore every mark of leprosy, they acted on the contrary word of Christ that declared them clean. Jesus considered them clean because of their faith; if he had thought otherwise, we can hardly believe he would have sent them to the priests. Those priests represented God's judgment; Christ received them as clean and therefore eagerly sent them to God as such.

Nonetheless the visual evidence testified that these men were not clean. Before healthy skin had begun to break through the horrible splotches, before their bodies lost the ravaging effects of leprosy, they were to accept that they were clean. So firm must their resolution be that what Christ had said was so, despite the contrary evidence, that they were not merely to enter into a nearby village, they were not merely to find some supportive family member, but they were to go to the priests to be inspected with regard to the presence of the leprous condition they displayed. That is what Christ was asking them to do, and that is what they set out for because of their faith. As the apostle Paul wrote, "We live by faith, not by sight" (2 Cor. 5:7), and in that manner these lepers proved the reality of their faith.

Charles Haddon Spurgeon rightly applies this example to the case of every sinner declared righteous and whole by the gospel of Jesus Christ:

> As these men were to start straight away to the priest with all their leprosy upon them, and to go there as if they felt they were already healed, so are you, with all your sinnership upon you, and your sense of condemnation heavy on your soul, to believe in Jesus Christ just as you are, and you shall find everlasting life upon the spot. This is my point, and it is of the first importance. Sinners, as sinners, are to believe in Jesus for everlasting life.[2]

All of this highlights an essential principle of Christian salvation. You do not wait until you are clean to come to God, but you come in your uncleanness to be made clean. You do not come to God after you have attained to righteousness, but you come unrighteous, to be declared just by the precious blood of Jesus. This is what the biblical doctrine of justification teaches: just as you do not cry out to Jesus on the basis of your supposed merits, neither are you declared just by God for the sake of your supposed righteousness. Even your best righteousness is, according to Scripture, nothing but a filthy rag (Isa. 64:6), hopelessly corrupted by the sin that is in you. As Romans 4:5 tells us, it is not the godly but the ungodly who are justified through faith in Christ: "To the man who does not work but trusts God who justifies the wicked, his faith in Christ is credited as righteousness." This is called imputed righteousness,

God crediting Christ's perfect righteousness to unrighteous sinners who trust in him.

If you try to come to God on the basis of your righteousness, you will be refused. For the salvation God provides is to sinners, to the wicked. But to these he gives the righteousness of Christ as a gift of grace that comes by faith alone.

I doubt that these ten lepers understood all of that. They had heard about Jesus; they saw him and called out to him. They then heard his reply, and with simple faith in him they went off to the priests. They would not have known the basis for their salvation, and yet it is clear, I think, that Jesus intended them to find out. I say this because of the ceremony the priests would be required to perform after declaring them to be clean.

I already referred to the portion of Leviticus dealing with leprosy, including the procedures for their examination and restoration to the people. Part of the restoration process included a specific sacrifice, found in Leviticus 14:4–7. This sacrifice provided one of the clearest Old Testament testimonies to the saving work of Jesus Christ.

The sacrifice involved two birds, each representing an aspect of Christ's work. One was killed, its blood drained into the pot, representing Christ's substitutionary death as an atonement for our sin. The other bird then was dipped in that blood, so that it now bore the stain of sin. That same blood was sprinkled on the person being cleansed, applying it and its benefits to him. Finally, the live bird, dipped in the blood of the one that had died, was released to fly far away out into the sky. We can well imagine the priest and the former leper, gazing up as that bird became smaller and smaller to their sight, the red mark harder and harder to see, the evidence of sin and God's judgment go-

ing farther and farther from their sight until it was gone altogether. Some of them, I am sure, would have thought of
the great statement of Psalm 103:12: "As far as the east is
from the west, so far has he removed our transgressions
from us."

It was God's wisdom that when a man who bore such
horrid testimony to sin and judgment as leprosy had all that
removed, on that occasion he should be confronted with
the gospel, the good news of the atoning work that takes
away our sin. It is no wonder then that we learn that many
of the priestly order eventually put their faith in Jesus (see
Acts 6:7), having dwelt so long among the clear gospel
preaching that was found in the Old Testament ceremonies.

All of this leads me to ask a question: On what basis are
you to consider yourself clean, really clean, whole, really
whole, just, really, truly just and righteous, when you are
confronted with daily evidence to the contrary? The answer is this: Because of the Word of God. On the basis of
the authority of God, the God, Paul says, "who gives life to
the dead and calls things that are not as though they were"
(Rom. 4:17). On the basis of the saving work of Jesus
Christ, who died for us that we might have new life in him.
You do it by trusting Jesus and believing the Scriptures,
which say to all who have come to Jesus for mercy: "You
were washed, you were sanctified, you were justified in the
name of the Lord Jesus Christ and by the Spirit of our God"
(1 Cor. 6:10). As the hymn says,

> Cast thy guilty soul on him;
> Find him mighty to redeem
> At his feet thy burden lay;
> Look thy doubts and cares away

Now by faith the Son embrace;
Plead his promise, trust his grace.

Furthermore, we note that though these men believed Jesus and went, it was while they were believing that the transformation took place. "And as they went," Luke records, "they were cleansed." This is something you will also find to be true. Yes, you are utterly incapable of cleansing your own heart, of healing your sin-sick soul. But you are commanded to trust Jesus Christ. What you will find is that as you trust him you are being changed. What you cannot do he will do in your life, in your heart, in your habits. It is his work to make you godly, spiritually alive, keen for the things of God. So come to Jesus just as you are, ungodly, barely penitent, worldly and hard of heart, weak in desire for spiritual things. "What must I do to be saved?" asks the sinner, and the Word of God consistently replies, "Believe in the Lord Jesus, and you will be saved" (Acts 16:31). He will save you through and through, even as you walk by faith in the way he has commanded. "And as they went," Luke records, "they were cleansed." So shall it be for you.

The Thanksgiving in which Christ Delights

We have now considered two points. The first was this cry for mercy that is always certain of a saving response. The second was this display of saving faith that rose above the evidence and received salvation from our Lord. The third and final point of our passage is this: the thanksgiving in which our Lord Jesus so greatly delights.

I began this chapter noting that this miracle gives us a broader view than most, because it so well presents our situation before salvation, which is guilt, during the actual coming of salvation, which is grace, and then afterward the result of that salvation, which is gratitude. Thus we have here a helpful summary of the Christian experience: guilt, grace, and gratitude. The last of these is brought to the fore in Luke 17:15–19:

> One of them, when he saw he was healed, came back, praising God in a loud voice. He threw himself at Jesus' feet and thanked him—and he was a Samaritan. Jesus asked, "Were not all ten cleansed? Where are the other nine? Was no one found to return and give praise to God except this foreigner?" Then he said to him, "Rise and go; your faith has made you well."

There are some who argue that verse 19 indicates that only this one grateful man received full salvation, that is, the salvation of his soul. You can see why, for only this one bore the fruit of gratitude and came back to Jesus. Obviously Jesus makes some distinction between the grateful man and the others. In verse 19, the New International Version reads that his faith had made him well, but in the Greek the verb is "to save." "Your faith has saved you," Jesus says, and so we might infer that the others were not saved because of their ingratitude.

But I do not think that meaning is intended. All ten of the lepers showed great faith. All ten were cleansed of leprosy, the great symbol of our sin. One of the main points I have been making is that salvation is by faith alone, and not by works. Justification does not depend on sanctification; gratitude therefore is a result of salvation and not its cause. If these nine cannot be saved because of ingratitude then I dare say very few of us could offer a convincing hope for heaven.

What this episode does depict is how little gratitude wells up to Jesus Christ in light of the enormity of what he has done. Think of these ten men! If only one of them had been a leper, they should have been overwhelmed with praise for such an incredible miracle. But all ten were lepers, and they all were cleansed. Imagine what an effect this had on their lives! It was like being given a new life. And yet only one out of ten came back to give thanks to the Lord!

Before we become too indignant, however, let us observe how well these nine represent us. We may not have been cured from leprosy, but we have been healed from the horrid state it represents. We who were guilty have been robed in Christ's holy dress. We have been born again, given new life, with power for righteousness and hope for eternity. So, when it comes to gratitude, how do we rate?

Let's peruse a few indicators, starting with prayer. Do we praise God in prayer? Do we thank him for our many blessings? For our health, for his provision, for instruction and fellowship, for a great purpose to life, for redemption and forgiveness and power for righteousness, for the resurrection of the dead? That's a lot to be thankful for! But isn't it true that our prayers are mainly lists of requests, even complaints, for things we want but have not received? I don't want to overstate this case. It is not wrong to bring our requests to God; indeed, it is the instinct of reborn children. Do not feel guilty for asking and for sharing your burdens with the Lord as they are. But are we thankful to him? Do we cast ourselves at his feet with joy, praising God with gratitude to Jesus Christ? If not, then we are as impoverished when it comes to spiritual riches as those nine who received their salvation and went upon their way.

What about our giving? Our willingness to serve, even

in menial ways, our zeal for the extension of the gospel, our kindness to others who are weak, our interest in and willingness to sacrifice for the missionary work of the church? Each of these is an outflowing of our gratitude to Jesus for this great salvation, and thus a measure of our spiritual attitude.

I want to stop now before I make you feel too guilty, because guilt is not the proper motivation for any of these Christian works. Our guilt was taken away at the cross. I would be glad, however, to quicken you to this high calling and privilege set before us by the Samaritan leper in this passage. His example shows us it is good to be grateful. Alexander Maclaren rightly waxes: "We increase the sweetness of our gifts by thankfulness for them. We taste them twice when we ruminate on them in gratitude. They live after their death when we bless God and thank Jesus for them all. We impoverish ourselves still more than we dishonour Him by the ingratitude which is so crying a fault."[3]

It is a blessing to us when we are grateful to Jesus; gratitude is the pump that primes our joy and the surest sign that we are really learning to know the love of God. But the greatest reason for our thanksgiving is the one so evident here—Christ's joy at the gratitude of his people.

It is always true that the greatest gift a bride can offer her love-smitten groom is the overflowing joy of her heart. And how troubling it obviously is to our compassionate Lord to see that his gifts mean more to us than he does. "Were not all ten cleansed?" he asked. "Where are the other nine? Was no one found to return and give praise to God except this foreigner?" And so you may ask—and well you should—what can I do to give pleasure to this my Lord and the Savior of my soul? The answer is here: give from your heart praise to God and thanksgiving to Jesus Christ.

only a Samaritan

There is a clear emphasis in Luke 17:16 on the nationality of this man. Luke tells us, "and he was a Samaritan," one of that nation so hated and shunned by the Israelites. Jesus says in verse 18, "Was no one found to return and give praise to God except this foreigner?" The point here is his lament that the Israelites, those most privileged in access to God, the nation that knew God's special care and blessing, all failed to give thanks and praise to God. How could that be, except that privilege had produced presumption and from that the bitter fruit of self-absorbed pride and unbelief.

There is good news associated with this Samaritan, because he shows us the universality of the gospel. This man was excluded from God's people and a stranger to God's covenant—"without hope," Paul says, "and without God in the world" (Eph. 2:12). And yet when he trusted in Christ and came to him with thanks, Jesus received him without prejudice: "Rise and go; your faith has made you well." Jesus indicates that the faith that cured the man is also the means of full fitness and spiritual health. It is by faith alone that we become well. But it is also a full confirmation of Jesus' joy at the faith and gratitude of this man, regardless of his background. As Paul, again, remarked: "Now in Christ Jesus you who once were far away have been brought near through the blood of Christ" (Eph. 2:13). No matter who you are, what you have been, you are fully accepted by Jesus Christ when you come to him in faith.

We need to note that this man who drew so near to Christ, who so thanked him with joy, was the one out of the ten who had been farthest from Jesus before these events. This man, as a Gentile, was very far from God. If he had gone to Jerusalem and tried to enter the temple he would have encountered a Keep Out sign directed against all foreigners. In-

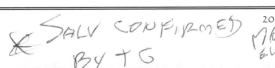

deed, the word used for that in the Greek, undoubtedly the word scrawled in warning on the barrier wall in the temple court, is the same one Jesus used to describe this man: *allogenes*, or "other nation." He was not of the people of God.

And yet, when confronted with the great reality the temple symbolized, the reality of Christ and his saving work, this outsider was the one who was willing, who was eager, who was motivated to draw as near as he could and to offer up a heart of thanks and praise. You see the point: the more we think we deserve from God, the better we think we are, the higher claim we think we have on God's mercy and provision, the less joy we will have as Christians and the less thanks we will offer up to God. This is why humility, with the fear of the Lord, is the key to spirituality, to thankfulness, and, yes, to joy. That is why the apostle James writes, "Humble yourselves before the Lord, and he will lift you up" (4:10).

We are infinitely unworthy of all his mercy, all his love, all his provision, and we might well be cut off from every such blessing without a shred of injustice. If we are in our right minds, if we are really healed and cleansed by the work of our Savior, then we will pour out our hearts in praise and thanksgiving, thus giving him such great pleasure and ourselves true blessing.

If we find ourselves weak it is likely because we are not thankful or conscious of our sin and therefore the extent of God's mercy to us. And if we wish to grow strong, to flourish in the things that matter, we will begin by repenting of our ingratitude, remembering our debt, returning to the Lord in humility, and pouring out our hearts with thanks to him who loves us so, who gave himself for us and reigns now for us in glory—even this same Jesus Christ. To him be the glory and the praise and the thanks, forever. Amen.

Sight to the Blind

Luke 18:35–43

*when he came near, Jesus asked him, "What do you want
me to do for you?" "Lord, I want to see," he replied.
Jesus said to him, "Receive your sight;
your faith has healed you." (Luke 18:40–42)*

Jesus made considerable use of contrasts in teaching his disciples, and Luke 18 is loaded with them. There is the well-known parable of the Pharisee and the tax collector, which contrasts two ways of approaching God—one by works and the other by faith. There are a number of figures for comparison, many of whom are models of faith. First there is the persistent widow who will not give up until she gets the help she needs. There are the little children, about whom Jesus says, "Unless you receive the kingdom like they do you will never enter it" (18:17). In obvious contrast is the

rich young ruler, who will not receive the kingdom with a
child's faith, who does not persist, who would not give up
his worldly treasures and therefore goes away unblessed by
his encounter with Jesus. Luke 19 begins with Zacchaeus,
in obvious contrast to the rich young ruler. Zacchaeus is
glad to find salvation in Christ and therefore gleefully gives
his money away to those he earlier had cheated.

The blind man in this passage is an important part of
these comparisons and contrasts. He has much in common
with Zacchaeus and also with the persistent widow. His
faith is the kind shown by the children, the kind that receives the kingdom. Negatively, he is contrasted with the
religious scholars and leaders who have been opposing Jesus, who do not see him for what he is despite having eyes
to see. In a striking way he is set against the rich young
ruler; here is a beggar who finds true riches. He is also contrasted with the crowds who were gathered around him to
watch Jesus as he passed by. In all of these contrasts, the
blind beggar—we are told in Mark's Gospel that his name
is Bartimaeus—despite his great poverty and brokenness
and sorrow, receives the greatest riches, wholeness and joy,
because he put his faith in Jesus Christ.

This is the last of our studies of the miracles and the
last that is presented in Luke's Gospel. What we find here
is a theme that comes across through all of the miracle accounts, namely, the great reversal that takes place through
faith in Jesus Christ. Jesus was fond of saying that the last
will be first and the first will be last, a teaching that occurs
five times in the various Gospel accounts. This is the contrast he has in mind, a great reversal empowered by his
cross and empty tomb. Those who trust in Jesus, though
lowly and weak and afflicted, will end up blessed. But
those who do not put their faith in him, however rich and

p 217

powerful and exalted in the world, end up poor and sorry
and rejected by God—if not in this world then in the age
to come.

The Blind Man

Our present study is not only the last of Jesus' miracles
in Luke's Gospel, but it serves well to sum up all we have
learned through our examination of these great saving
works. One of the points I have been making is that the
miracles show us far more than random acts of kindness on
the part of our Lord Jesus. They show us more than that he
was a nice sort of fellow, willing to help out when and as he
could. They present for us, rather, an advertisement of the
scope of his redeeming work. They direct us to him with his
divine power as the One who is willing and able to save sinners. They offer to our minds and our hearts a foretaste, a
sneak preview, of all that will be when finally death is put
away and Satan is disarmed, when sin and sickness are no
more, and God will wipe every tear from the eyes of his
people.

To that end, the various afflicted people in the miracle
accounts represent what the reign of sin and of Satan
means to fallen humanity. They are a portrait gallery of sin
and its effects. Leprosy shows sin's corrupting power and
condemning presence. The lame show sin's debilitating
power. The dead proclaim the wages of sin; the demon-
possessed show the destructive domination that is always
the result of our bondage to sin and to Satan.

In all of our miracles, however, there is one kind of malady we have not yet encountered but which is central to
the Bible's depiction of humanity in sin. That malady is
blindness. Perhaps Luke saved this for last, passing by other

earlier examples for the sake of emphasis, so important is this portrait for our understanding of what it means to be lost in sin.

In the Bible, sight is synonymous with belief. Jesus' famous words to Nicodemus tell us this: "I tell you the truth, no one can see the kingdom of God unless he is born again" (John 3:3). Spiritual regeneration by the Holy Spirit is correlated, therefore, with the receiving of sight. Receiving the gift of faith by the grace of God is perhaps best expressed by the hymn "Amazing Grace," which says, "I . . . was blind but now I see."

Conversely, the apostle Paul writes of spiritual blindness as a key element of Satan's dark rule. It is the "dominion of darkness" (Col. 1:13). Writing in 2 Corinthians 4:4, he says, "The god of this age has blinded the minds of unbelievers, so that they cannot see the light of the gospel of the glory of Christ, who is the image of God." Those who are unable to receive Jesus Christ as Savior and Lord therefore are people who lack a vital faculty; they are, like the blind man, unable to see.

This means everyone who is not a Christian is blind to a great and beautiful and saving reality, namely, the love of God in Jesus Christ. People think that unbelief, that atheism or its various cousins, is sophisticated and intellectually superior. But unbelief is blindness to the greatest of all realities—blindness to the glory and power and holiness of God whose presence is everywhere revealed. Though they are victimized, they are not helpless victims, for their blindness is willing and active. They have rebelliously suppressed the truth God has revealed even in nature (Rom. 1:18), and so they are blind to the realities of eternity, to heaven and hell, and worst of all blind to the One who came to redeem us from our sin by his blood.

This is the difference between Christians and others. It is not that Christians are spiritually superior, more spiritually attuned or willing, but that by his grace God has opened our once blind eyes. Otherwise we would be just like the depraved and deceived people around us. Therefore, when Christians encounter people on the streets or in the workplace who are oblivious to the things of God, utterly unconcerned with spiritual realities, our response should be not contempt but pity for their sakes. Our pity should spur us to greater zeal for the gospel, which is the light God has given for the opening of eyes that are blind.

The Blind Man's Cry

It is a blind man who figures in this last miracle account, and there are four things I want to observe from this passage, beginning with his cry to Jesus.

Jesus was on his way to Jerusalem and was passing through Jericho, about twenty kilometers to the northeast. Luke's narrative has focused on his journey to the cross ever since chapter 9, where he writes, "As the time approached for him to be taken up to heaven, Jesus resolutely set out for Jerusalem" (v. 51). We are now very close to his entry into that city, which takes place in the next chapter, and also to Jesus' last days before his death.

Luke tells us a crowd was watching Jesus, as there always was, a crowd who had heard of his mighty works in other places, who were surely curious if this would be the one to throw off the Roman yoke. They were no doubt anxious to see what the notorious Jesus of Nazareth looked like, and this blind beggar heard the great commotion. He asked what was happening and they told him, "Jesus of Nazareth is passing by" (Luke 18:37).

With that little information, the blind man began yelling: "Jesus, Son of David, have mercy on me!" What a great contrast there was between this man and the crowd! The people gathered there were curious; to them this was something along the lines of entertainment. The passing of Jesus was a sight to see, something to talk about later. Some of them would have been chatting among themselves, while others perhaps spoke out in praise of Jesus. This crowd anticipates the one he would soon encounter in Jerusalem, so there were probably cries of "Hosanna!" But to this crowd, he was a teacher, an example, a political reformer, a challenge to the system, and people who think of Jesus that way, who think of him as an object of discussion rather than a Savior, will never cry to him as this blind man cried, "Jesus, have mercy on me!"

That was the right response to Jesus' passing, and yet the people tried to quiet him. Luke 18:39 tells us, "Those who led the way rebuked him and told him to be quiet." The Revised Standard Version has it that it was those who stood in the front of the crowd who said this, rather than Jesus' procession, and I think that is a more likely translation of the Greek. Those in front tried to quiet the noisy blind man; themselves nothing more than an audience, perhaps even an appreciative one, they didn't want the spectacle disturbed. Little did they realize that this is the cry sweetest to Jesus' ears. It was not as an entertainer or an aloof statesman that Jesus came into the world but as a Savior for those who cry, "Son of David, have mercy on me!"

Blind Bartimaeus was not thwarted by the crowd's rebuke, but, as verse 39 goes on to say, "He shouted all the more, 'Son of David, have mercy on me!'" This cry, "Son of David," is one that obviously identified Jesus in his messianic office. There is ample evidence that this was a catch-phrase for the promised Messiah. For instance, in Luke 20:41, Jesus' statement that the Messiah must be the Son of David was immediately accepted as true by the teachers of the law.

One scholar says about the use of this title: "Son of David points to Jesus as the royal Messiah in the line of David. As such he fulfills the promises God made to David regarding the eternal reign of David's offspring (2 Sam. 7:12–16), and he acts as the unique agent in bringing the rule of God to the earth, a rule that is characterized by salvation and blessing."[1]

This was the very thing Jesus' miracles were intended to reveal, and this man, though blind, understood what nearly everyone else around him did not. Obviously he had heard about Jesus and especially about his power to heal and make whole. Undoubtedly it was because he so well recognized his own need that he connected what he heard about Jesus with the promises of God to send a Messiah who could help people like him. Perhaps he had long dwelt upon and now remembered what was foretold of the Messiah:

> The Spirit of the Lord is on me,
>> because he has anointed me
>> to preach good news to the poor.
> He has sent me to proclaim freedom
>> for the prisoners
>> and recovery of sight for the blind,
> to release the oppressed,
>> to proclaim the year of the Lord's favor.

Those were the words Jesus used, reading from the Isaiah scroll, to announce his ministry (Luke 4:18–19). As always, it was the poor, the afflicted, the blind who saw Jesus for what he was, who believed what was promised of him in the Scriptures and revealed in his miracles.

Jesus Stopped

Despite the efforts of the crowd to quiet him, the blind man was heard by Jesus. Luke 18:40 says, "Jesus stopped and ordered the man to be brought to him."

Here is a marvelous scene. Jesus had his face set to Jerusalem, now drawing so near. There was a cross on his mind, a great struggle that cast its shadow back upon his path. Surely he was bracing himself, focusing on what was to come. If there was ever a time when we might understand Jesus ignoring the needs of yet another afflicted soul it was now. And yet, however absorbed with the great affairs that rested upon his shoulders, the work before him that would be the focal point of all human history, Jesus stopped when he heard that cry: "Jesus, Son of David, have mercy!"

First notice that whatever the crowd was calling out to him did not stop him. Their empty words of praise had no more impact on Jesus than empty, formal worship does today. Their comments and opinions were of no concern to him then, just as the appraisal of unbelieving scoffers gives him no pause today. But the cry of a single believer in need of help did stop Jesus. "Jesus stopped," we read, and in those two words is a wealth of riches.

Jesus is able to do what no earthly minister can. However attentive a pastor may be to his flock, he still can do only one thing at a time, be at one only place, give his attention to only one thing at a time. It is sadly true of every earthly minister that he sometimes will be unavailable to pay attention to your need. But what is true of all others is never true of Jesus Christ.

Jesus is now in heaven, and we find in Scripture that he has fairly extensive duties. He is administering the universe, guiding and empowering his church, wielding providence, and serving as executor of the grand plan of God. Meanwhile he is receiving the praise of a vast host beyond counting. And yet, when you cry to him for mercy, for help, for comfort, for him, you receive his whole attention. He stops, as it were, for you. Though his human nature is finite, he possesses as well an infinite divinity so that he can lavish his attention upon each and all who cry out to him. And he does that without taking his attention off of any of his other sheep or his vast divine duties.

Those who treat Jesus as a spectacle, as an object of discussion, receive from him nothing; but for the cry for mercy he stops and gives the whole of himself.

Jesus ordered Bartimaeus to come forth. Mark's Gospel gives us more detail here than Luke does: "Jesus stopped and said, 'Call him.' So they called to the blind man, 'Cheer up! On your feet! He's calling you.' Throwing his cloak aside, he jumped to his feet and came to Jesus" (Mark 10:49–50). What a model of faith this blind man is! He heard that Jesus was passing by and wasted no time calling out to him. Then when called forward he sprang to his feet, he cast aside his cloak—probably spilling all the money he had received through begging—and raced out to Jesus. Surely he knew he might not get another chance like this one. In all those things he shows what we must do if we would be saved—cry to Jesus as he is being proclaimed, throw off every encumbrance, every hindrance that might keep us away, and race to him who calls us. J. C. Ryle comments:

Let us strive and pray that we may have like precious faith. We too are not allowed to see Jesus with our bodily eyes. But we have the report of His power, and grace, and willingness to save, in the Gospel. We have exceeding great promises from His own lips, written down for our encouragement. . . . Let us trust those promises implicitly, and commit our souls to Christ unhesitatingly.[2]

If you want to be saved, you, like Bartimaeus, must give no heed to what other people think or say. You must recognize your great need as a blind sinner and race forward to the Lord Jesus Christ, who calls all who will believe to come and be saved. First he cried to Jesus, then when called he came at once.

"Cheer up! On your feet! He's calling you!" cried the crowd, turned by Christ into agents of the gospel. We in the church have the privilege of serving that same cause now, for all who never have come to Jesus. "Come," we must cry to the world, "all who are blind, guilty, and unrighteous, poor in spirit and lost in sin. Come to Jesus, for this is the day he is calling you to be saved!"

Willing to Give

What happened next is more astonishing still. Luke tells us, "When he came near, Jesus asked him, 'What do you want me to do for you?' " (Luke 18:40–41). His question is the third point for us to notice.

I have to ask myself, "What would I do if this happened to me, if a blind beggar stepped forth asking me for mercy?" I would pray for him, asking God to give him grace in his obviously difficult condition and if it were his will to alleviate this man's bodily suffering. I would discuss various social services and tell him how our church might minister to him. But the one thing I would never do is to casually ask him, "What would you like me to do?" What he really wants I cannot do!

We have here a clear sign of Jesus' divinity, that he should ask so audacious a question to a man who so obviously wanted a miracle. Jesus, who reads the hearts of men, saw the faith that brought this man forward. He saw in advance the desire for the light of so great a healing. And because he is able, as the Son of God come to heal and to save, Jesus could say so invitingly, "What do you want me to do for you?"

One of the reasons we don't often draw near to Jesus, don't cry out to him in prayer for our needs, is that we easily forget what he is able to do. We forget his ability to oversee our affairs and to minister with power to the heart of faith. It is true that his will and not ours governs his sovereign power. I thank God that our Lord does not answer my every prayer; I lack the wisdom, much less the omniscience, to know what is good for me. The Scripture therefore promises answers when we pray in God's will (1 John 5:14).

There are many prayers that are manifestly in God's will, and yet we seldom pray them. "Lord, give me strength to turn from sin." "Lord, help me to flee this temptation." "Lord, give me a heart to love the things you love." And then there is the prayer offered up by this man, the simple prayer so overflowing with faith, "Lord, I want to see."

Suppose you had Jesus make the kind of open offer Bartimaeus received. What would you ask for? If you are wise, your request would have nothing to do with lottery tickets or popularity or romance or worldly success. If you know yourself and your real need, if you know this world in which you live and its real issues, and if you know anything of Jesus Christ and his glory, then you would pray for none of those things. "Lord," you would cry, "I want to see! Lord, heal me of my blindness, take away my sin, give to me your salvation, and show yourself to me!"

What an astonishing question Jesus asked of Bartimaeus, but of course he already knew what Bartimaeus wanted. And when we come to him in faith, wanting the things he wants for us, he places within our hand the key to his chest of treasures just as he did for Bartimaeus. Jesus is not a cosmic genie, not a lamp for us to rub and manipulate. But he is an all-loving giver of grace. He is the Lord, who is able to give with power, who is willing to give for salvation and new life. "What would you like me to do?" is a question and an offer Jesus genuinely makes to those who look to him in faith.

One of the great studies in Scripture is to peruse what are called the "I Wills" of Christ. Here you will find promises that he is sure to fulfill if you will only ask. "Come to me, all you who are weary and burdened, and I will give you rest" (Matt. 11:28). That is a promise, and you will find it true. "Never will I leave you," he says, promising to be your constant Savior. "Never will I forsake you" (Heb. 13:5). He promises to be our light, so that we can see (John 8:12). He promises new life for those who ask, saying, "Whoever believes in me, . . . streams of living water will flow from within him" (John 7:37). He says, "Whoever drinks the water I give him will never thirst" (John 4:14).

Of course, Jesus' greatest promises have to do not merely with this life but with eternity. "Whoever acknowledges me before men, I will also acknowledge him before my Father in heaven" (Matt. 10:32). And then there is the promise that is our greatest hope: "Everyone who looks to the Son and believes in him shall have eternal life, and I will raise him up at the last day" (John 6:40). In all these and more, Jesus says to the heart of faith, "What do you want me to do?" If we will ask for these, he will surely give.

Sight Given and Received

"Lord, I want to see," the man cried. First he cried out for mercy, then he came, and then he asked this of the Lord. And how wonderful it is to read, "Jesus said to him, 'Receive your sight; your faith has healed you'" (Luke 18:42). There is power! When Jesus began speaking his reply, Bartimaeus was as blind as he had been all along. But by the time Jesus had finished speaking, light was streaming into and through his eyes. That is the kind of power Jesus wields for salvation.

This is the fourth thing for us to notice, that this blind man did receive his sight from Jesus. If you have never put your faith in Jesus Christ, you have available to you a transformation as radical, as instantaneous, as the one that gave sight to Bartimaeus. What matters is not the extent of your problem but the infinity of Christ's power, not the depth of your sin but the height of his grace. If you will believe, if you will cry out to him, you too will see, just as this man opened his eyes and found himself looking into the face of his Savior. Indeed, if you will be so bold as to admit your sin and the blindness it brings, to agree that Jesus is the Savior sent from God, to cry out for his help and come to him in faith, you will have forgiveness and life everlasting on the spot.

But how, you may ask, can a blind man see? How can I, a sinner, seek righteousness? How can an enemy of God seek his favor? The answer is by faith, which is the gift of God. By accepting his offer of pardon. By receiving the free grace that glorifies him so. How could Bartimaeus, whose eyes were blind, see with the eyes of his heart, but that God was shining his own light there? Indeed, it is God's special pleasure to give sight to the blind, to give legs to the lame, to give righteousness to sinners, so that in all these salvation might be by his grace alone, and therefore to the glory of his name. "I praise you, Father, Lord of heaven and earth," Jesus once cried out, "because you have hidden these things from the wise and learned, and revealed them to little children. Yes, Father, for this was your good pleasure" (Luke 10:21).

All the other people in that crowd failed to see the most important thing about Jesus. They had physical sight, but they lacked spiritual insight. The reason is that they did not seek the things of God from God. They trusted instead to their own wisdom and blind presumption. It pleased God therefore to give spiritual sight to the blind while the others though seeing should be blind to the greatest of realities. That is why they did not see what the blind man saw, that Jesus of Nazareth, the worker of wonders, was also the Son of David sent to be Messiah and Lord. Those who will not seek from God will not find; those who will not ask will not receive.

Bartimaeus cried out, he came, he asked, and finally he received his sight. "Your faith has healed you," Jesus said. Literally, he said, "Your faith has saved you" (Luke 18:42). So it was, for we see Bartimaeus following after Jesus and giving praise to God, which are the two signs and results of salvation that comes through faith. That is the great principle of Christianity, that we are saved and healed by faith in Christ and that alone.

Of course, it was Christ who healed him; his faith merely brought him to the Savior. Jesus' point is that faith is the condition necessary for salvation. Alexander Maclaren writes, "The condition is for us, the power comes from him. My faith is the hand that grasps His; it is His hand, not mine, that holds me up. My faith lays hold of the rope; it is the rope and the Person above who holds it, that lift me out of the 'horrible pit and the miry clay.' My faith flees for refuge to the city; it is the city that keeps me safe."[3]

The Great Reversal

The case of this man presents the great reversal that is central to what Christianity is all about. Those who are happy are those who started sad but came to Jesus. The same is true for the poor who become truly rich, the weak who become really strong, those rejected by men who are fully accepted by God. All this because Jesus is mighty to save, because he came to seek and to save those who were lost.

When we come to Jesus in faith, this great reversal is applied to us. We who have been rebels against God are received as beloved children. We who have sinned are forgiven, because Jesus paid our debt; we who are guilty receive the righteousness of him who bought us with his blood. We who were blind are made to see; we who were weak receive the power of Jesus by the indwelling Holy Spirit; we who were dead in sin are now alive in Christ.

But it was only this blind man, in all that great crowd, of whom these things could be said. He alone cried out for mercy and came forth in faith. That is the contrast that Luke sets before us in this chapter. We are asked to consider which we will be as Jesus passes by, as his gospel is proclaimed. Will we be the religious leaders sitting in judgment on him in their petty self-righteousness? Luke's Gospel makes clear that those will never be accepted by

Spectators

God. Will we be the consumers in the crowd, thinking only of our entertainment, seeking only some diversion for the day? If we are, then Jesus will soon pass by, leaving us without a Savior on the day of God's wrath.

Or will we be like this man, once blind, who though with every natural disadvantage possessed the one thing needful, which is faith in Jesus Christ? He alone humbled himself before God, sought hope from God's Word and thus received faith to perceive the Savior. He alone, though blind, could see his salvation. So he called to Jesus, he came to Jesus, he asked of Jesus, and by faith in Jesus he was saved. Seeing Jesus, trusting him and following after him, the man who was blind entered the kingdom of light, the kingdom of God, leaving behind the kingdom of darkness. It is this kind of transformation, this great reversal, that all the miracles of Jesus point to. It is a salvation that is available to us. And yet so few will seek it.

One Grand Miracle

We began our studies of the miracles with C. S. Lewis's observation that they are only rightly understood when they are seen as part of one grand miracle that is the coming of Jesus Christ. That is the great supernatural event, of which the various miracles are but particular manifestations. So it is here in our last miracle. With his coming Christ opens the eyes of those who were blind to the knowledge of God. His coming reveals God to the eyes of our faith, even as he said, "Anyone who has seen me has seen the Father" (John 14:9).

If there is anything we should see, therefore, in all these mighty works, it is the need of humankind for a Savior and the readiness of Christ to save us to the uttermost. The miracles show us the futility of our works; they turn our gaze away from anything that comes from our own power, while directing our eyes to Jesus Christ, who is mighty to save. He is the One, as he foretold in the synagogue at Nazareth, anointed to preach good news to the poor, sent to proclaim freedom for the prisoners and recovery of sight for the blind, to release the oppressed, and to proclaim the year of the Lord's favor (Luke 4:18–19).

His work therefore will be sufficient for all our need and is worthy of the whole of our trust. To him be the glory forever. Amen.

Notes

chapter 1: The Meaning of the Miracles

1. C. S. Lewis, *Miracles* (New York: Touchstone, 1996), 143.
2. Alfred Edersheim, *The Life and Times of Jesus the Messiah* (Peabody, Mass.: Hendrickson, n.d.), 451.
3. Darrell L. Bock, *Luke 1:1–9:50*, 2 vols., Baker Exegetical Commentary on the New Testament (Grand Rapids, Mich.: Baker, 1994), 1:442.
4. John Calvin, *A Harmony of the Gospels, Matthew, Mark and Luke*, 3 vols. (Grand Rapids, Mich.: Eerdmans, 1972.

chapter 2: "I Am Willing"

1. John Calvin, *A Harmony of the Gospels: Matthew, Mark and Luke*, 3 vols. (Grand Rapids, Mich.: Eerdmans, 1972), 1:244.
2. Charles Haddon Spurgeon, "And Why Not Me?" in *The Parables and Miracles of Our Lord*, 3 vols. (Grand Rapids, Mich.: Baker, 1993), 2:59.

chapter 3: Authority to Forgive

1. D. Martyn Lloyd-Jones: *I Am Not Ashamed* (Grand Rapids, Mich.: Baker, 1953), 38.

2. A. W. Tozer: *God Tells the Man Who Cares* (Harrisburg, Penn.: Christian Publications, Inc., 1970), 20.
3. Donald A. Hagner, *Matthew 1–13* (Dallas: Word, 1993), 232.
4. J. Gresham Machen, *Christianity and Liberalism* (Grand Rapids, Mich.: Eerdmans, 1923), 117.

chapter 4: "Just Say the Word"

1. C. S. Lewis, *Mere Christianity* (New York: Macmillan, 1958), 109, 112.
2. A. W. Tozer, *God Tells the Man Who Cares* (Harrisburg, Penn.: Christian Publications, Inc., 1970), 138.
3. R. C. Sproul, *A Walk with Jesus* (Ross-shire, Great Britain: Christian Focus, 1999), 119.
4. Ibid., 119–20.
5. Alfred Edersheim, *The Life and Times of Jesus the Messiah* (Peabody, Mass.: Hendrickson, n.d.), 545.
6. Charles Haddon Spurgeon, *The Miracles and Parables of Our Lord*, 3 vols. (Grand Rapids, Mich.: Baker, 1993), 1:479–80.

chapter 5: Weep No More

1. Martin Luther: *Sermons of Martin Luther: The Church Postils*, ed. John Nicholas Lenker, 8 vols. (Grand Rapids, Mich.: Baker, 1983), 5:146–47.
2. Ibid., 5:146.
3. Geerhardus Vos, *Grace and Glory* (Carlisle, Penn.: Banner of Truth, 1994), 49.
4. Thomas Watson, *A Body of Divinity* (Carlisle, Penn.: Banner of Truth, 1992), 296, 297.
5. Charles Haddon Spurgeon, *The Miracles and Parables of Our Lord*, 3 vols. (Grand Rapids, Mich.: Baker, 1993), 1:50.

chapter 6: Lord of the Storm

1. Donald A. Hagner, *Matthew 1–13* (Dallas: Word, 1993), 222.
2. Charles Haddon Spurgeon: *The Parables and Miracles of Our Lord*, 3 vols. (Grand Rapids, Mich.: Baker, 1993), 1:121.
3. J. C. Ryle, *Mark* (Carlisle, Penn.: Banner of Truth, 1985), 83.

chapter 7: Humanity Restored

1. M. Scott Peck, *People of the Lie* (New York: Simon & Schuster, 1983), 176.
2. Ibid., 168.
3. Charles Haddon Spurgeon: *Miracles and Parables of Our Lord*, 3 vols. (Grand Rapids, Mich.: Baker, 1993), 1:545.
4. Darrell L. Bock, Luke 1:1–9:50, 2 vols., Baker Exegetical Commentary on the New Testament (Grand Rapids, Mich.: Baker, 1994), 1:777–78.
5. William L. Lane, *The Gospel of Mark*, New International Commentary on the New Testament (Grand Rapids, Mich.: Eerdmans, 1974), 187.

chapter 8: Tears and Laughter

1. J. C. Ryle, *Holiness* (Durham, England: Evangelical Press, 1979), 273.
2. J. C. Ryle, *Luke* (Wheaton, Ill.: Crossway, 1979), 113, 114.
3. Darrell L. Bock, *Luke 1:1–9:51*, 2 vols., Baker Exegetical Commentary on the New Testament (Grand Rapids, Mich.: Baker, 1994), 1:805.

chapter 9: Feeding the Five Thousand

1. William L. Lane, *Mark* (Grand Rapids, Mich.: Eerdmans, 1974), 229.
2. Charles Haddon Spurgeon, *Miracles and Parables of Our Lord*, 3 vols. (Grand Rapids, Mich.: Baker, 1993), 1:558–59.

chapter 10: Miracles and the Cross

1. I. Howard Marshall, *The Gospel of Luke*, The New International Greek Commentary (Grand Rapids, Mich.: Eerdmans, 1978), 389–90.
2. Alexander Maclaren, *Expositions of Holy Scripture*, 10 vols. (Grand Rapids, Mich.: Eerdmans, 1959), 6:15–16.
3. Martin Luther, WA 5.165.39–166.1; see Alistair McGrath, *Luther's Theology of the Cross* (Oxford: Blackwell, 1985), 152.
4. Dave Dravecky, *Hope in the Midst of Adversity*, www.lifestory.org, n.d.

chapter 11: Opposition to the Miracles

1. See Mark 9:38; Josephus *Antiquities* 8.45–49.
2. See Graham Twelftree's discussion of these in *The Dictionary of Jesus and the Gospels*, ed. Joel B. Green and Scot McKnight (Downers Grove, Ill.: InterVarsity Press, 1992), 167–68.
3. C. L. Sulzberger, *New York Times*, 8 October 1958.
4. Jonathan Edwards: *Christ Exalted*, from *The Words of Jonathan Edwards*, 2 Vols. (Peabody, Mass.: Hendrickson, 1998), 2:215.
5. Augustine *On the Trinity* 13.15.19, in *Mark*, ed. Thomas C. Oden and Christopher A. Hall, Ancient Christian Commentary on Scripture (Downers Grove, Ill.: InterVarsity Press, 1998), 45.
6. J. C. Ryle, *Luke* (Wheaton, Ill.: Crossway, 1997), 160.
7. Alexander Maclaren, *Expositions of Holy Scripture*, 11 vols. (Grand Rapids, Mich.: Eerdmans, 1959), 5:122.
8. C. S. Lewis, *Mere Christianity* (New York: Macmillan, 1943), 56.

chapter 12: One Who Gave Thanks

1. Martin Luther, *Sermons of Martin Luther: Church Postils*, ed. John Nicholas Lenker, 8 vols. (Grand Rapids, Mich.: Baker, 1983), 5:66–67.
2. Charles Haddon Spurgeon, *Miracles and Parables of Our Lord*, 3 vols. (Grand Rapids, Mich.: Baker, 1993), 1:74.
3. Alexander Maclaren, *Expositions on Holy Scripture*, 11 vols. (Grand Rapids, Mich.: Eerdmans, 1959), 6:130.

chapter 13: Sight to the Blind

1. D. R. Bauer, "Son of David," in *Dictionary of Jesus and the Gospels*, ed. Joel B. Green and Scot McKnight (Downers Grove, Ill: InterVarsity Press, 1992), 766.
2. J. C. Ryle, *Mark* (Carlisle, Penn.: Banner of Truth, 1985), 223, 224.
3. Alexander Maclaren, *Expositions of Holy Scripture*, 11 vols. (Grand Rapids, Mich.: Eerdmans, 1959), 6:104–5.

Index of Scripture